Faithful Investing

The Power of Decisive Action and Incremental Change

Edited by James W. Murphy

CHURCH
PUBLISHING
INCORPORATED

In memory of my sister, Dr. Anne Marie Murphy Janca,
who taught me to become a better person a little bit more each day

———————

Church Publishing
19 East 34th Street
New York, NY 10016
www.churchpublishing.org

Cover design by Jennifer Kopec, 2Pug Design
Typeset by Rose Design

A record of this book is available from the Library of Congress.

ISBN-13: 978-1-64065-244-6 (paperback)
ISBN-13: 978-1-64065-245-3 (ebook)

Contents

For additional resources and reference materials, including a brief "History of the Interfaith Center on Corporate Responsibility (ICCR)," please visit this book's website: www. churchpublishing.org/faithfulinvesting.

Foreword

Money—how we use it, how we manage it, how we relate to it—is an intrinsic part of our lives as individuals, organizations, and yes, faith communities. Jesus certainly recognized this. More than two hundred verses in the gospels deal with money and our relationship to it.

An important part of relating to and managing money involves how we invest it for both the short and long term. Many of our religious institutions have been blessed with financial gifts over the years which, through prudent investment and market returns, have grown into significant endowments and other permanent funds which help support current and future ministries. Those individuals who are charged with overseeing these funds clearly have a fiduciary duty in making investment decisions but, more and more, recognize their moral, ethical, and religious responsibility in determining how and where their money should be invested. In response to these core beliefs, the market has developed a variety of socially responsible (SRI) and environmental/social/governance (ESG) options. There are also approaches that exclude investing in certain industries, e.g. fossil fuels, or emphasize active shareholder engagement and corporate advocacy. These issues are complex and there are no easy solutions. How does a religious organization become a faithful investor, while, at the same time, ensuring that the funds entrusted to its care and custody generate returns and income to support mission and ministry for years to come?

That is what this book is all about. It doesn't provide the answers but will help faith communities begin to reflect, discern, and consider various investment approaches and options that incorporate moral, ethical, and faith-based values. It is written by a group of thoughtful and faithful Christian experts who are sharing their knowledge, thoughts, and ideas to support our faith communities as they engage in God's mission in the world within their own unique situation and context. I commend their work to you as you continue on this journey.

This book is also an ecumenical collaboration among financial leaders from various denominations. Discussions around money and investments clearly transcend theological and ideological differences and provide innovative ways for new partnerships. We hope that this effort will spark other creative opportunities.

Finally, this book reflects the clear reality that much like worship, formation, education, and outreach, managing money is a critical and important ministry of the Church. Keep this in mind as you tackle the various issues raised and discussed. May you be filled with God's grace and blessings as you embark on this important work.

—Donald V. Romanik
President, Episcopal Church Foundation

Introduction

James W. Murphy

Again, it will be like a man going on a journey, who called his servants and entrusted his wealth to them. To one he gave five bags of gold, to another two bags, and to another one bag, each according to his ability. Then he went on his journey. The man who had received five bags of gold went at once and put his money to work and gained five bags more. So also, the one with two bags of gold gained two more. But the man who had received one bag went off, dug a hole in the ground and hid his master's money. After a long time the master of those servants returned and settled accounts with them. The man who had received five bags of gold brought the other five. "Master," he said, "you trusted me with five bags of gold. See, I have gained five more." His master replied, "Well done, good and faithful servant! You have been faithful with a few things; I will put you in charge of many things. Come and share your master's happiness!" The man with two bags of gold also came. "Master," he said, "you entrusted me with two bags of gold; see, I have gained two more." His master replied, "Well done, good and faithful servant! You have been faithful with a few things; I will put you in charge of many things. Come and share your master's happiness!" Then the man who had received one bag of gold came. "Master," he said, "I knew that you are a hard man, harvesting where you have not sown and gathering where you have not scattered seed. So I was afraid and went out and hid your gold in the ground. See, here is what belongs to you." His master replied, "You wicked, lazy servant! So you knew that I harvest where I have not sown and gather where I have not scattered seed? Well then, you should have put my money on deposit with the bankers, so that when I returned I would have received it back with interest. So take the bag of gold from him and give it to the one who has ten bags. For whoever has will be given more, and they will have an abundance. Whoever does not have, even what they have will be taken from them." (Matt. 25:14–29 NIV)

This is a difficult passage for many, but always a reminder to me that each of us is accountable for the actions we take as church leaders. Nowadays, an increasing number of Christian faith communities (local, judicatory, and denominational) as well as religious orders (Episcopal, Orthodox, Roman Catholic, and others), schools, and many other religious institutions are seeking to invest their assets in socially responsible (SRI) or environmental/social/governance (ESG) options. This choice can be a complex issue for the many volunteers on church investment and endowment committees, as well as for governing boards, who grapple with numerous strategic decisions on a regular basis. Many of these investment volunteers, and even some of the professionals involved, do not have the expertise to make such complex decisions on their own, and need to spend significant time and energy reviewing their investment goals and strategy before they move forward.

In recent years, more and more congregations and religious institutions are asking how they can invest for their future, growing their endowed and other invested funds, while also focusing on their values and making the world, nation, and their local communities healthier, more vibrant, and more equitable in a number of ways. This book attempts to bring leading experts and practitioners from across the denominational spectrum to offer their wisdom and experience on these topics so that the lay and ordained leadership of our congregations/organizations can discern decisive steps forward, taking into account their context, particular needs and goals, capacity, and financial resources. We hope that this book will help religious leaders better understand many of the issues, challenges, and opportunities involved in seeking to make their investment choices reflect their faith-in-action, not only to resolve their desire to "do something," but to help them be empowered for action in their context. We do not cover every topic, but seek to share basic information and to include several topics of current interest.

However, this book and its many resources and insights are not intended to instruct your congregation or institution on what you *must* do. Rather, they are intended to raise your awareness of the many questions and opportunities you should consider for what is best strategically for your congregation/organization. There are a great number of factors to consider: the size of your endowment, your comfort with risk and potentially limiting diversification, the potential extra cost of investing in this way, availability of denominational resources for investment, suggestions and sometimes directives on investments from our various denominational bodies, agreement among individual church leaders on strategic investment choices and how to measure results, or investment choices such as engagement or exclusion, and many more issues, in addition to any legal restraints on the assets in question. The intention of this book is to empower your leaders to reflect on the steps you can and should take within your particular context, and those choices may be *not* to take any action at all at this time.

As each situation will be unique, this book will help educate your leaders to consider what actions are appropriate for you, and based upon that, to take decisive actions, usually incrementally, that reflect your values as a congregation or organization. As leaders who actively reflect on these issues, you should *not* consider a lack of action or a delay of action necessarily as a weakness. Incrementally moving to where you wish to be in the future is a powerful choice and one that honors the complexity of your congregation/ organization and the importance of being good stewards of the assets you oversee. Rushing to be "perfect," however one defines that, may well be the enemy of the good, as you will read later.

In fact, some congregations/organizations may decide after reading this book that they do not wish to invest in any of the ways described. SRI requires discipline and intention and some methods may not be appropriate for all. For example, most Roman Catholic parishes are not legally capable of holding endowments for themselves, but perhaps parishioners would seek to encourage their bishop or diocese to do so with assets they may hold (see case study 3 from Catholic Extension). Additionally, an organization which either cannot or does not have its own investment assets may choose to create a type of impact investment, such as starting a local revolving loan fund out of its annual budget or encouraging constituents to invest in a manner that would satisfy SRI goals.

For many entities that do have assets to invest, they may or may not be able to hold individual stocks, or may have a variety of other issues within their circumstances. All of the contributing authors seek to share insights and wisdom that they have collected through their careers, some of which are multiple decades long, and to offer reflections on how and what you may consider, and potentially act on. Not all of our readers will agree with the individual perspectives of our contributors, but we offer this variety of voices to provide a broad overview of historical, practical, and innovative perspectives.

Clearly there is a very diverse set of voices in this book. This has been intentional from the beginning of this work. It is our belief that no single denomination, organization, or individual has all of the best answers when it comes to the topic of investing, and certainly each of us can learn much from our other Christian "cousins" and their experiences. Roman Catholic institutions may invest differently in some ways from Unitarians, and some congregations may be free not to follow their national churches, yet many will wish to stay closely in step. This book is not intended to judge actions taken/not taken or to prescribe conformity on how you should invest, but to be an accessible first step for a very diverse audience.

From the earliest discussions of this book, the intention has been to create a unique text from the perspective of multiple denominations and not simply focus on what the Episcopal or Presbyterian or even what certain multidenominational institutions or collaborations have accomplished on their own. In this new era when denominational affiliation is less and less important to many individuals, I hope that this book will be a positive sign for potential collaboration in other ways in the future. I hope that this book's example of denominational generosity, by sharing a variety of stories, insights, and expertise from various Christian traditions, can demonstrate how denominations can share strengths, and weaknesses, so as to work together in more effective and practical ways. We do not all need to agree on everything to further God's kingdom here on earth, especially if that betterment is done incrementally. Do families or successful business enterprises require conformity on doctrine before they accomplish great things? Of course not! Finding new opportunities for collaboration between denominations to solve problems, share resources, and learn from each other through concrete projects like this book should be an important goal of all of our various traditions, in our view, leading to more opportunities for eliminating the wasted energy from each denomination always trying to "recreate the wheel" only for themselves.

The contributors and editors of this book have sought to be as inclusive as possible in their use of terminology when referencing communities of faith, knowing that there is such a wonderful diversity among different denominations, and even *within* them (this is so true within the Episcopal Church). Any reference that might not capture how your tradition may reference itself or its leaders is not meant to exclude you; it is simply not possible to satisfy all the different ways that these aspects are expressed.

There will be many references throughout this book to socially responsible investing (SRI) as well as several other similar or related activities, environmental/social/governance (ESG) investing, impact investing, community investing, exclusionary screening, impact investing, shareholder activism, etc. Although these terms are different from one another, they all fall under that wider umbrella of the variety of activities most people bring to mind when "SRI" is referenced. I hope that this book will be many things to different people, and should not be the end of your journey but the beginning (or perhaps a continuation) for the reader of your own empowerment.

Addressing a common misperception, some people may feel that SRI is anticapitalist. I would certainly not agree with that assessment and, to the contrary, would argue that actions reviewed in this book are clear demonstrations of how investors and members of our free society and market-based economy are actually seeking to protect and grow their investments and make our society in the United States, and throughout the world, better and more equitable. Actions discussed in this book were done with deep faith and conviction over the course of many years. These actions have enhanced the lives of many throughout the world, and in so doing will in time also benefit the long-term value of the investments being held by the thousands of religious entities throughout the world.

I offer deep thanks to all of the contributors to this book: their work was tireless and I am deeply grateful not only for their willingness to share their insights, but also for their patience and collaboration with me as I edited and adapted their texts, seeking to pull together a helpful volume on this very broad topic. Special thanks to Greg Rousos, Katie McCloskey, and Byrd Bonner, who all helped so much in the early stages of planning this book.

Seeking to keep the individual voices intact from our wonderful choir of contributors, readers may notice that some historical facts about the movement of SRI may be repeated in multiple chapters. Though not all socially responsible topics are covered in this book, a good selection of common subjects were chosen, and we hope that they make this volume a good primer, overview, an inspirational recapping of a unique history, and a useful toolkit for beginners. Additionally, the focus of this book is on Christian institutions and leaders as our main audience. Due to that focus, we regret not being able to include the wise perspectives and important insights of our non-Christian brothers and sisters. We are aware of the great work that many Jewish and Muslim leaders have done in SRI. Perhaps in a future volume!

(I also apologize to our non-US readers, as I know some Canadians and other international church leaders may be reading this book and saying, "Hey, Jim, what about us?" I regret that we were not able to address any issues that would be different regarding SRI or other investment guidelines for our wonderfully progressive neighbor to the north, or for any other countries on our fragile earth.)

I also express tremendous gratitude to our publisher, Church Publishing Incorporated, for all of their staff's wonderful guidance and insights. Thank you as well to Donald Romanik, the president of the Episcopal Church Foundation, for his consistent support throughout the creation of this book and the support of my endowment/planned giving colleagues and others at ECF. Special thanks to Josh Zinner and the leadership at the Interfaith Center on Corporate Responsibility (ICCR), all my colleagues at the other denominational foundations and denominational entities who helped in our work, my insightful friend Christopher Rowe at the Church Pension Group, and Marcia Shetler, the executive director of the Ecumenical Stewardship Center, for your willingness to help connect me to many of the denominational collaborators on this book. "We, who are many, are one body in Christ, and individually we are members one of another" (Rom. 12:5).

CHAPTER 1

Basic Concepts and Terms*

Greg Rousos, William Somplatsky-Jarman, and Aimee Moiso

Introduction

This chapter provides background and objectives on socially responsible investing (SRI), including its purpose and impact. There are many different definitions and implementations of SRI. There is much to learn about this type of investing for all of us and many different ways to implement it. This is yet another way that Christians might engage in healthy, productive, and effective ways to be witnesses to their values and faith.

This book is not intended to prescribe a singular approach to socially responsible investing but to assist the reader in defining and implementing socially responsible investing within their particular context. On various issues one might find Christians with different perspectives. As you examine socially responsible investing, the same is true. Well-intentioned Christians will have different perspectives on how to implement socially responsible investment. That is all right. Investors will have different financial and human resources available that might dictate how the investor approaches socially responsible investing. The means, context, and many other factors are all considerations. Our hope is that this book empowers the reader to take the necessary steps to invest in a manner consistent with their values.

Background

One could make the case that socially responsible investing has been around for several hundred years. While there were no publicly traded financial stock markets and investment securities for these types of investments in centuries past, people and organizations made certain that their purchases

---

* This material, including organizations and websites noted, is provided for informational purposes only and should not be viewed as an endorsement or as investment, tax, or other professional advice.

and participation with companies comported to their values. For example, there were some religious denominations that prohibited involvement with the slave trade. In the late nineteenth century, some denominations and church members began to view investments in tobacco and alcohol companies as forbidden. As publicly traded gambling companies emerged, they often joined the forbidden list of "sin stocks." Just prior to World War II, some churches raised concerns about the social consequences of investment policies.[1] While this is barely considered socially responsible investing by today's standards, it certainly demonstrated organizations making financial and other decisions based on values possessed by the organization.

Socially responsible investing (SRI) really started to attract a following in the 1960s due to the variety and intensity of social issues. These issues included civil rights, urban decay, gender equality, and the Vietnam War. During this time two approaches emerged. One saw faith-based organizations and individuals joining civil society appeals to corporations, banks, and investors, including faith-based institutions, to invest in solutions to societal problems such as community economic development, affordable housing, job training, etc. The second involved using the rights and opportunities of investors to influence corporate policies and practices.

The other learning over time was the value of the collaborative work among denominations and organizations. Examples are the Corporate Information Center and the Interfaith Committee on Social Responsibility in Investment that had been incubated at the National Council of Churches of Christ (USA) starting in 1971. In 1974, the Interfaith Center on Corporate Responsibility (www.iccr.org) was formed by Protestant denominations, and shortly thereafter the National Catholic Coalition for Responsible Investment (NCCRI) came on board.

Denominations, including their foundations and to a lesser extent pension funds, were active and considered leaders with socially responsible investment. In 1963, a Presbyterian Women delegation returned from South Africa noting the extensive presence of US corporations. They urged advocacy with those corporations to oppose apartheid, and if the corporations were unresponsive, to consider divestment. Apartheid would galvanize the social justice advocates, including church members, throughout

---

1. For a useful summary of the history of early efforts to engage corporations through direct citizen appeal and through investor action, see *Social Responsibility & Investments* by Charles W. Powers (Nashville: Abingdon Press, 1971). Additional history can be found in *The Field of Social Investment* by Severyn T. Brown (New York: Cambridge University Press, 1991).

the decade. A seminary student–led petition drive called for banks not to renew a revolving credit facility with South Africa, foreshadowing future campaigns to end all bank loans to the country. Years later, churches in Europe and the United States would urge international banks serving on a committee to negotiate repayment of South Africa's short-term debt. The banks were pressed to extract substantial funds from the country, a result widely credited as contributing significantly to the end of apartheid. The first religious shareholder resolution was filed in 1971 by the Episcopal Church calling for General Motors to withdraw from South Africa until apartheid was ended.[2]

While South African apartheid prompted considerable activity by faith-based investors, it was not the only issue addressed. The United Church of Christ, United Methodist Church, and Unitarian-Universalists called upon major oil companies to change policies, and participated in an effort to increase job opportunities at companies for African Americans.

In the area of *community investment*, several denominations created programs to invest in community economic development designed to make capital available to underserved communities and peoples. Although a much broader topic, efforts like this often invest or loan capital to economically disadvantaged communities (see chapter 8). A primary tool of community investment is microfinance. Microfinance loans are typically for those that do not have access to conventional banking services and provide a small amount of money to individuals to start or expand a business. The World Council of Churches captured this idea in 1968 when they developed the concept of ethical investments that foster peace and solidarity.[3] This concept came to life when a variety of church denominations formed the Ecumenical Development Cooperative Society (now known as Oikocredit International) in 1975 to invest in cooperative enterprises in impoverished areas.[4] In 2018, it had over $1 billion invested with 693 cooperatives globally.[5]

As religious organizations became more deeply involved in socially responsible investing and aware of the opportunities to witness to their theological

---

2. "History of ICCR," Interfaith Center on Corporate Responsibility, accessed May 20, 2019, *https://www.iccr.org/about-iccr/history-iccr*.

3. "1968," Oikocredit, accessed May 20, 2019, *https://www.sasr.oikocredit.coop/k/en/n7303/news/view/103736/106017/1968.html*.

4. "History," Oikocredit, accessed May 20, 2019, *https://www.oikocredit.coop/about-us/history/history*.

5. "Oikocredit's Portfolio and Member Capital Grow as It Implements Updated Strategy," Oikocredit, accessed May 20, 2019, *https://www.oikocredit.coop/k/n2613/news/view/305096/9049/oikocredit-s-portfolio-and-member-capital-grow-as-it-implements-updated-strategy.html*.

and ethical values through using the rights afforded them as investors, the need for setting policies on socially responsible investments became clear. Several denominations developed policies affirming this commitment, which were adopted officially at national meetings. The Presbyterian Church (USA) denomination adopted a policy at its General Assembly in 1971. The policy statement [including] a discussion about investments being "an instrument of mission and includes theological, social and ethical considerations."[6] The basis for this belief is that all are stewards of God's resources and therefore, "We confess that the Lord is really the acknowledged Master of our entire life—moral, physical and material."[7] Faith-based investors benefit from such denominational policies of socially responsible investing and other social justice issues as they inform ethical and moral action and provide opportunity for reflection and further action.

Theological Understanding of Socially Responsible Investing

When Christians think about justice and ethics, we often begin from our awareness of situations around us that are unjust. Things that seem not right in the world are easy to spot—from trash along our sidewalks or smog in our air to neighbors sleeping in cardboard shelters or refugees fleeing on rickety rafts. When we consider faithful ways to invest our money, we might similarly think first of things we don't want to support. In contrast, in this section we will begin by imagining what kind of world the God of life wants for us and for those we share it with. What are the characteristics and traits of that world? How are we committing all of our lives—including our money and investments—to participating in the creation and continuation of that world?

In 2012, the World Council of Churches (in which many denominations contributing to this volume hold membership) issued a call for an economy of life, justice, and peace for all. The call bore witness to God, who affirms the goodness of the whole Creation and who created human beings as part of a larger web of life: "The whole community of living organisms

---

6. *Corporate Social Responsibility Investment Policy Guidelines*, adopted by the 183rd General Assembly of the United Presbyterian Church (USA) in 1971, *https://www.presbyterianmission.org/wp-content/uploads/mrti_ga_policy_-_19711.pdf*.

7. *The Corporate Witness of the General Assembly Presbyterian Church in the United States 1976*, approved by the 116th General Assembly of the Presbyterian Church in the United States and adopted by the General Assembly Mission Board on March 20, 1976, *https://www.presbyterianmission.org/wp-content/uploads/mrti_ga_policy_-_19761.pdf*.

that grows and flourishes is an expression of God's will and works together to bring life from and give life to the land, to connect one generation to the next, and to sustain the abundance and diversity of God's household."[8] This verdant, interdependent, and relational description of Creation sprouts with vibrant verbs: grow, flourish, bring life, give life, connect, sustain. Keeping these energizing words about God's hope for the world in the forefront of our minds and hearts helps theologically and faithfully orient our conversation about socially responsible investing.

Many of our churches primarily take charitable approaches to issues like poverty and hunger: we donate to food pantries and shelters or send our members on mission trips to build houses and paint schools. Our Christian faith does call us to care directly for our neighbors in need, yet our faith also calls us to ask what causes inequality and injustice. The systems around us—political, economic, financial, etc.—do not exist in a static state. They are human made, and therefore both corruptible and changeable and even (dare we say it?) redeemable. Socially responsible investing pushes us to think theologically about how systems can contribute to the flourishing and sustenance of life.

Christians are also called to consider how the power of our voices and our money can promote a more just world that provides for the flourishing of all. Investing and divesting can themselves be acts of advocacy, but they are strengthened when coupled with prophetic speech that supports life-giving action and decries that which is life-denying. As investors, we can speak against systems that exacerbate inequality and injustice. The prophets raised their voices against the exploitation of workers and those who are most vulnerable, ceaselessly clamoring for change to the systems that enriched the few while impoverishing the masses. In Luke 18, Jesus tells a parable of a persistent widow who will not give up asking a judge for justice, until finally he relents. The parable implies that God is on the side of the widow and of all who continue to cry out for just solutions. Those of us with the power to speak and advocate do so on behalf of our neighbors who often go unheard. In the case of investments, our money gives us power as shareholders to affect how companies do business, and how businesses treat employees, communities in need, and even the earth itself.

---

8. "Economy of Life, Justice, and Peace for All: A Call to Action," World Council of Churches, paragraph 2, last modified July 19, 2012, *https://www.oikoumene.org/en/resources/documents/wcc-programmes/public-witness-addressing-power-affirming-peace/poverty-wealth-and-ecology/neoliberal-paradigm/agape-call-for-action-2012/economy-of-life-justice-and-peace-for-all?set_language=en.*

In Matthew 6, Jesus teaches his followers about putting their heart and soul into that which gives life: caring for others without expecting accolades, seeking daily bread for oneself and one's neighbor, investing in treasures of heaven rather than those that can be corrupted and lost, and seeking God's will on earth. This kind of "investing" is echoed in Colossians 3, where disciples are called away from greed, deceit, and malice, and are summoned to clothe themselves in what gives life to relationships and communities: compassion, humility, gentleness, and forgiveness. In our decisions about financial investments, we demonstrate our faith when we support institutions and corporations that promote strong and healthy civil societies, ethical and equitable practices, and the common good. As followers of Jesus, we express what we believe with our whole lives, including the pocketbook and Public Square. Not all will agree on processes or what will be most impactful, but taking the time to reflect and make value-based choices is key.

Finally, socially responsible investing requires us to be honest with God about the ways in which we as churches and individuals may have put our financial well-being above the summons of our faith. Too often, the bottom line—not our deepest convictions—has governed our financial decision-making. We have frequently accepted economic systems and contexts as "givens" rather than as constructs that can be questioned and challenged. We often acquiesce to models of greed, consumption, and competition rather than resisting their destructive and exploitative influences. We live in God's good Creation, and share stewardship of this world's sustenance and flourishing. Our limited imagination has not always propelled us toward creativity and innovation in that mission. Yet a Christian approach to socially responsible investing necessarily requires a measure of repentance and lament for how we have not lived up to the calling of our faith. All we are and all we have belongs to God. In assurance of God's grace and empowering Spirit, we can commit ourselves anew to envisioning and investing in a vibrant, flourishing world of hope and life for all.

Common Understandings

Before getting deeper into socially responsible investing, we want to establish a common understanding and use of major concepts and words. The investment concepts in this book are relatively basic, and there are books that explain the broader disciplines of investing more comprehensively. But a few definitions and explanations are warranted.

The primary party related to investments is the *investor*. An investor is the party with assets that they wish to invest in a company. An investor places money in a company such that the investor's money can grow over the long term. The growth or the return on the investment creates wealth over time. Companies seek investors as a source of capital or funds. The company uses these funds to invest in or grow the company's business. In this book, a *security* references a stock or bond of a company and is often used interchangeably for a *stock* or a *bond*. By owning a stock, also known as an *equity*, the investor is considered a *shareholder* because the investor has a share of the ownership of the company. The shareholder is entitled to certain privileges, such as voting on resolutions and filing shareholder resolutions, depending on the type of stock security. An investor that purchases a bond, also known as a *fixed income security*, acts as a lender or creditor to a company. The company owes the investor the amount of the bond and pays the investor interest at a rate noted on the bond. The name *fixed income security* is based on the bond paying interest at a fixed rate and amount over the life of the bond. A collection of securities is considered an investment *portfolio*; portfolios are normally formed for a particular purpose or objective, such as growth, stability, income production, etc. Securities are grouped into classes with similar characteristics such as nature and size. Examples of *asset classes* include cash, equities, fixed income, commodities, real estate, and others. A subset of asset classes is known as a *sub-asset class* where securities are grouped according to even more characteristics, such as larger and smaller companies, international, etc. The purpose of asset classes and sub-asset classes is to assist in determining the *asset allocation* (or the choice of how much to invest in one asset or sub-asset class) of the portfolio. For our readers just beginning to delve into these issues, the contributors of this section are focusing on the most commonly used assets for most religious institutions. A further description of sub-asset classes is found in chapter 2.

Investing Assets

With this very basic understanding of securities, an investor can begin to consider the best way to invest their assets in securities (or pooled funds, discussed below). An investor or entity should consider the amount of risk they are willing to accept, their liquidity needs, and their time horizon. *Risk* is defined as securities that might have volatile performance and a risk of significant decline or increase in value. A method used to manage risk is to implement a *diversified portfolio*. A diversified investment portfolio might include many different types of sub-assets of stocks, bonds, and other asset types. The common wisdom is that the more diversification in a portfolio, the less risk in the portfolio. Your professional investment advisors will be able to help you create a diversified portfolio.

Liquidity relates to an asset or security and the degree to which it is marketable or available for purchase or sale, and if the purchase or sale affects its price. *Readily marketable securities* is a term used for assets that are available for purchase or sale in a relatively short time period. An asset or security that is liquid is readily marketable and allows an investor to receive cash in exchange for their investments or assets as needed. This is important if the investor has upcoming obligations for which they need to have cash available. *Time horizon* is the length of time that an investor will keep assets invested. Longer-term investments allow assets to recover from negative performance. The longer the time frame to hold an investment, the more risk the investor can accept because securities have more time to recover if there is a market downturn.

An investor must determine their risk, liquidity, and time horizon prior to investing the assets. The investor should document these considerations so that the portfolio is implemented in ways consistent with these considerations. Such documentation is usually included in an *investment policy statement*, or IPS. The investment policy statement should include an *asset allocation*, which directs the percentage of assets to be invested in stocks and bonds as well as further allocations to various types of stocks and bonds (e.g., large- and small-cap, etc.) and should clarify ranges for allocation in all asset and sub-asset classes. This statement also clarifies if there are some asset classes that are to be avoided. Also included in an IPS are the investor's objectives related to socially responsible investing. The investment policy statement provides an investor or their advisor with a road map and policy on how to implement the portfolio. More discussion on investment policy statements is included in the next chapter. Please see this book's appendix for samples of IPSs.

Pooled Funds

While a stock or bond security is an investment in a specific company, investment vehicles can also pool several securities into a single investment so that an investor can purchase a pool of securities instead of purchasing each security individually. The pool of securities is referred to as *pooled funds*, and can include stock securities, bond securities, or a combination of them, in addition to many other types of assets, including other funds. Examples of pooled funds include mutual funds, exchange traded funds, hedge funds, private equity funds, and proprietary common or commingled funds, such as those available from many denominational and other secular sources. The benefit of pooled funds is that an investor does not have to select individual securities and manage the portfolio since the pooled funds are already constructed on the investor's behalf. An investor should make sure that the pooled fund meets their investment objectives prior to placing assets in the pooled fund. Pooled funds normally charge fees, sometimes called an *operating expense ratio*, but there can also be other fees, such as for management, that an investor should consider and that decrease investment performance.

Pooled funds afford numerous benefits to the investor. In many cases, an investor that has less than several million dollars cannot achieve the investment diversification needed to mitigate risk in the portfolio. Without significant dollars to invest, the investor cannot own sufficient number of shares of each company's securities to make investing cost effective. The cost to trade smaller quantities (also called *lots*) of securities can be very expensive. This is where pooled funds offer significant advantages. An investor with even a small amount to invest can invest in a pooled fund. This allows the investor to achieve the necessary diversification and professional investment management with one investment in a pooled fund. There are equity, fixed income, and balanced pooled funds that allow investors to invest in a pooled fund that aligns with their desired asset allocation. Pooled funds that are balanced hold both equity and bond securities with varying asset allocations. Pooled funds will *rebalance* their investment holdings (reallocate between different types of securities) to their policy asset allocation. If the investor finds a pooled fund that matches their policy asset allocation, the investor will *not* need to concern themselves with rebalancing their portfolio, as the pooled fund will rebalance for them.

There are several considerations that an investor should know about pooled funds. The pooled fund investment manager or advisor is responsible for all investment decisions and activities of the pooled fund. An investor in a pooled fund does not have the ability to include or exclude particular securities in the pooled fund. The pooled fund investment advisor votes all proxies and files any shareholder resolutions for companies in the pooled fund. The investor in the pooled fund cannot determine screens, or vote proxies and file shareholder resolutions. That said, there are numerous pooled funds that are socially responsible (or have ESG factors included in investment decisions as will be described later). The pooled funds that implement socially responsible investing do so based on pooled funds' criteria, not that of the investors. A socially responsible investor should closely examine pooled funds to ensure they meet the investment objectives, including social responsibility.

Pooled funds are an effective investment option for many investors, including socially responsible investors. An important investment consideration is choosing between not investing in a socially responsible pattern or fund, and being a witness and an active socially responsible investor. For many investors, investing is a witness to one's faith and values, and is a powerful testimony. Being an effective witness can be accomplished through investments in pooled funds. However, certain investors might wish to be more active investors by selecting securities to be included or excluded from the portfolio, proxy voting on resolutions, and filing shareholder resolutions. This may only be accommodated by implementing a portfolio that holds individual company securities and not a pooled fund. Please know and recognize that there is not a right or wrong answer. Both approaches can provide powerful statements about the investor's faith and values. Every congregation/organization needs to take the time to review their investment needs and capacity for making investment decisions, as well as their own strategy for mission, before finalizing these important initial decisions. Few congregations/organizations have the means to invest directly in individual stocks, and do choose to invest in pooled funds through their denomination's or other secular options.

Measurement

There are several measures to understand an investment portfolio's performance. The most widely used is the investment's *return*, which is the amount the investor earns from their investments from both yield (income and dividends) and appreciation of the value of the assets. The investment return is often calculated net of fees, which is the investment return less the cost and fees associated with the investment. In order for the investor to evaluate their portfolio's performance, the investor can compare their investment to an *industry standard benchmark* that is similar in asset allocation. An investment return that is greater than the benchmark indicates that the investment portfolio is performing well. Other investment portfolio measures include those involving measures of risk such as *beta* (the measure of the portfolio's volatility as compared to the broader market), *volatility* or return variations (measured by standard deviation of the annual rate of returns), and other more technical investment measures.

Fees can differ based on investment strategies. *Passive* or indexed investing, using pooled funds of a variety of kinds, focuses on securities that are consistent with a benchmark. By mirroring a benchmark, an investor hopes to receive the benchmark's return. The fees or costs of passive investing are low. The other strategy an investor may employ is *active management.* Active management attempts to outperform the benchmark due to actively researching investment opportunities. Active management typically has higher fees than passive investing due to more research and work involved. Calculating returns net of fees takes into consideration how the portfolio is invested, which is important due to the different strategies (active or passive) and different fees.

A potential challenge for socially responsible investing is measuring portfolio investment performance against a benchmark. While there are numerous benchmarks available, in many cases it is difficult to find a benchmark that may match a socially responsible investing portfolio. Due to the possibility of custom negative and positive screens employed in socially responsible investing portfolios (which will be discussed below), comparable benchmarks may not exist. Therefore, evaluating performance against a benchmark might be skewed due to the securities that are excluded or included in the investment portfolio and differ from the benchmark.

Shareholder Responsibilities

Companies hold annual meetings where shareholders elect company directors, ratify selection of auditors, consider other management proposals, and vote on any shareholder proposals. Usually the CEO will review the company's performance and may outline plans for the future. The board of directors updates shareholders at the annual meeting on the company's past performance and plans. Shareholders can speak at these meetings on matters related to the company. This allows direct shareholders to have a voice if they desire.

If the investor owns certain types of stock securities, they are entitled to vote on *resolutions*, proposals submitted addressing a particular issue to be voted on at an annual meeting that set policy for or provide direction to the company's board of directors. The resolutions are put forth by the company or by other shareholders. Shareholder voting on resolutions is an important aspect of shareholder participation in corporate governance and referred to as *proxy voting*. At times, shareholders might submit a resolution for proxy voting, which is referred to as a *shareholder resolution* (see chapter 4 for a more detailed explanation). A shareholder submits their resolution to the company's board of directors according to the rules of the Securities and Exchange Commission (SEC). The board of directors is responsible for reviewing the resolution. The board can decide whether to include the resolution in the proxy document sent to shareholders, along with their support "for" or "in opposition" to the resolution. If the board does not want to include the resolution, and believes there are SEC rules to support their position, they can request a ruling by the SEC. The shareholder can submit a response citing why the resolution should be allowed. The SEC will review the case and issue an opinion on whether the resolution should or should not be included. If the ruling favors the shareholder, the board will usually include the resolution along with a statement of opposition. Shareholders weigh the issues and positions and decide how they will vote. Shareholder resolutions are advisory and not binding on the company's board of directors, so even if they receive a majority vote, the board can ignore them. However, resolutions that receive a significant vote will often receive media attention. This encourages action by the company that speaks to shareholder resolutions being a crucial part of proper corporate governance procedures (see more in chapters 4 and 7).

Socially Responsible Investing Introduction

Defining socially responsible investing is difficult, as there is a myriad of considerations and alternatives. The best we can do is to explain the various considerations such that an investor can discern how or if they will implement particular socially responsible investing options in their portfolio. There are three main considerations for socially responsible investing. The first consideration is whether to screen securities or determining whether securities are included or excluded from the portfolio. Second, the investor should consider the level of advocacy they wish to have with companies in their portfolio. Last, *community/impact investing* is a consideration of socially responsible investing that seeks a positive social impact. An investor can choose to participate in one, two, or all of the aspects of socially responsible investing. As a person or people of faith, the investor must consider that they have a relationship with a company as an owner or creditor and that by investing in the company, the investor is supporting and is associated with that company's activities. Only the investor can decide their level of participation in socially responsible investing and how best to take action in their context. These considerations of socially responsible investing are used by both secular and religious investors. For Christians, each of these takes root in theological and biblical convictions. Scriptural admonitions like the Ten Commandments can provide a starting point for considering what we might resist investing in, such as companies that create weapons of war, do not pay their workers a living wage, or seek to gain from mass incarceration.

Security Screening

Security screening is often the first consideration of socially responsible investing. Some might consider screening as the only aspect of socially responsible investing, although many investors take a much broader and comprehensive view. Security screens are positive or negative depending on the investor's objective.

Positive screens identify securities to include in the investment portfolio. A frequent example of positive screens are environmental, social, and governance screens, often referred to as ESG screens. The objective of positive ESG screens is to identify companies that have good policies and practices in relationship to environmental, social, and governance issues.

Environmental concerns relate primarily to protection of the planet or caring for Creation. The effects of climate change on the planet have increased the sensitivity to investing in companies that promote positive initiatives that care for the planet (see chapter 7). Social concerns include diversity, pay equity, human rights, and consumer protection. Investors concerned with social issues focus on companies that care for people and community. A company's policies and practices are dictated by its governance structure. Governance includes the responsibilities and authority of management, the board, and the stakeholders. Governance concerns include board and management structure, executive compensation, and employee relations.

For many socially responsible investors, ESG screens are sufficient to demonstrate their faith and values by investing in companies with good practices. One might refer to these companies as good corporate citizens that take care of the environment, their community, and their employees while having sound governance models. There are firms and software that score companies on ESG metrics and can assist investors in discerning the companies to invest in based on the investor's criteria. Over the years ESG investing has grown dramatically, as many favor positive screens over negative screens. Certain investment professionals believe that companies with good ESG practices will last longer and be more profitable over time due to the improved practices compared to other companies.

Negative screens exclude companies from the portfolio. Investors have used negative screens for many decades. Typical reasons for excluding a company from a portfolio include the investor not wanting to profit from a company's activities or simply not agreeing with the company's products, services, policies, or actions. Negative screens are applied to a specific company or to an entire sector. One factor to consider when choosing to divest from a company is that the investor loses their ability to influence a company's policies and practices. By not holding the security, the investor is not entitled to vote on resolutions, file shareholder resolutions, and participate in the company's annual meeting. For these reasons, not all investors are in favor of divestment.

Some faith-based institutional investors take a nuanced approach that views screening a particular company as the last step after all engagement on a significant concern has failed to produce a positive change. For categories of stocks such as alcohol, gambling, tobacco, for-profit prisons, or pornography, negative or proscriptive screens may be more appropriate, as the company's basic business is the issue of concern. A faith-based investor's response will be informed by their theological perspective on involvement in the world as well.

There are many pooled funds that implement stock screening. There are not nearly as many pooled funds that hold bonds that invest both socially and responsibly. While an investor is a creditor when owning a bond and not an owner of a company, the investor should still consider their socially responsible investing objectives and apply those objectives to bonds as well as stocks. Socially responsible investors should consider implementing their objectives in the entire portfolio, not just the stock or bond portion of the portfolio.

Advocacy

The next aspect of socially responsible investment is advocacy. Advocacy includes voting on company resolutions, filing shareholder resolutions, and participating in company annual shareholder meetings. Shareholders should take seriously their responsibility to engage with a company through advocacy (see chapter 4).

Resolutions are presented to shareholders that set company policy and governance, and elect directors. This is a very important aspect of social responsibility, as resolutions could involve board diversity, pay equity, environmental care, and other social concerns. When shareholders do not vote, the outcome of the shareholder voting process usually conforms to the company's recommendations. Shareholders should consider voting as company recommendations may or may not be consistent with the shareholder's socially responsible values.

An investor that places their assets in a pooled fund is not able to vote on company resolutions. The pooled fund will vote company resolutions based on the pooled fund's policies. This does not allow an investor in a pooled fund to speak on a company's issues. An investor should consider the pooled fund's policies on voting company resolutions prior to investing in the pooled fund to determine if they are consistent with the investor's values. The pooled fund's policies are contained in the pooled fund's prospectus and other documents. An investor should always read a prospectus prior to investing in a pooled fund. As discussed above, while the investor will not have influence on pooled fund's policies, the investor can still find and invest in pooled funds that reflect and are a witness to the investor's values and faith.

Through advocacy, an investor can encourage a company to be inclusive, seek diversity, be equitable, care for creation, and act in the best interests of their community and employees. In recent years, shareholders have voted on resolutions that involved important issues such as human rights, corporate accountability, health care, environmental responsibility, and more. The holistic approach to socially responsible investing includes advocacy and screening. The goal is that investors are advocates to encourage companies to become better community citizens. However, if companies are unwilling to change, investors have the option to screen those companies out of their portfolio if the companies are not consistent with the investor's values. On a more positive note, an investor can reward a company that shares that investor's values by investing their assets with the company.

Community Investment and Development

What we, as contributors, would call community investment is another important aspect of socially responsible investing. *Community investing/ investment* can also be thought of as positive investing, social investing, or some combination thereof. The objective is to have a positive impact on the community, people, and the environment. The investor's focus shifts from a financial return to a social return, most often with the investor willing to accept a lower financial return on the investment, or a sole focus on community improvement over financial return. Many readers may be more familiar with the term *"impact investing"* (see chapter 8).

A community or positive investment implements programs such as microfinance, community programs, improved infrastructure, and environmental care. The risk associated with community investments is usually greater than an investment in a corporation, as the community investment is made in areas that are experiencing economic and/or social challenges. (Case study 5 highlights a positive investment in a school in the nation of Colombia.) Community investment can have a positive and dramatic impact on communities, the environment, and people's lives. In fact, some investors have chosen community investment as a positive approach to change instead of simply divesting of corporations that do not match their values. For some congregations, direct lending locally and other practices are an important part of how they engage in SRI, as a part of their overall efforts, or if they choose not to or cannot invest their assets in SRI vehicles.

Socially Responsible Investing Considerations and Challenges

As with all things, there are considerations and challenges when implementing a socially responsible portfolio. A major consideration that is discussed later in this book is that it is nearly impossible to implement a socially responsible portfolio that meets *all* the investor's objectives. That should not deter an investor from attempting to invest in this manner. An investor should start with a socially responsible investing approach that begins to accomplish the objectives, and the investor can continue to refine this approach over time.

The amount of diversification in a socially responsible portfolio must be considered, as that can impact the portfolio's risk and return. Traditional exclusionary investing that eliminates securities and sectors of the market thereby limits the universe of available securities. As noted earlier, diversification is an important investment technique to manage portfolio risk. There are methods to compensate for the reduced diversification, but it is best to work with a professional investment advisor to understand alternatives.

Numerous investment options are available through denominational foundations and other resources noted in the appendix of this book.

There are many theories on the impact that socially responsible investing has on investment portfolios. One such theory is that socially responsible investing will outperform, as the companies in a socially responsible investing portfolio have improved environmental, social, and governance policies and practices. However, an alternative theory contends that socially responsible investing limits the investment universe with negative screens, which in turn reduces diversification and increases risk in the portfolio. (See the various case studies on congregations and other entities.) While there are different theories, it is hard to compare a socially responsible portfolio to a standard portfolio. The screens and activities related to a socially responsible portfolio might alter the asset allocation, security selection, and fees. One can look to broad market indices to make general comparisons. Recent benchmark returns of the MSCI KLD 400 Social Index had an annualized return of 15.04 percent over 10 years[9] compared to the S&P 500 (TR) Index of 15.32 percent[10] over a 10-year period ending April 30, 2019. The returns are very close. Ultimately the investor must consider and determine for themselves if investing according to their values is important for potentially sacrificing non-SRI market returns.

Another consideration of socially responsible investing is the implementation of the portfolio. The investor must determine how to select securities based on positive and negative screens. For example, if the objective is to screen tobacco from the portfolio, the investor must define those companies to exclude. Does the investor determine the companies to exclude based on their revenue from that activity or product or some other measure? If the measure is revenue, should the percentage of revenue be 20 percent, 40 percent, etc.? The same consideration applies for positive screening in determining the companies to include in the portfolio. The investor must define the proper metric to identify the companies to include or exclude from the portfolio (see chapter 3).

The cost of implementing a socially responsible portfolio can be a significant consideration. There are additional efforts that go into implementing and managing a socially responsible portfolio that screens securities and/or

---

9. MSCI KLD 400 Social Index (USD) Fact Sheet, as of April 30, 2019, *https://www.msci.com/documents/10199/904492e6-527e-4d64-9904-c710bf1533c6.*

10. S&P Dow Jones Indices, as of April 30, 2019, *https://us.spindices.com/indices/equity/sp-500.*

engages in advocacy. This additional effort translates into *cost*, which means the fees associated with the portfolio might be higher than a non–socially responsible investing portfolio. The investor should consider fees and determine the proper approach for themselves, as fees can greatly impact the total return of an investment.

Depending on the investor's time and expertise, the investor may wish to implement a socially responsible investing portfolio through a pooled fund. Pooled funds are normally an easier, and more cost effective, way to implement a socially responsible investing portfolio, especially for religious organizations. However, as noted above, pooled funds may have their challenges. Most significantly, the investor must agree with the pooled funds' definition of socially responsible investing and how they select securities, vote resolutions, and engage with companies. Some pooled funds may add an extra layer of fees to the portfolio that the investor should consider, but offer various other benefits as previously described.

Trends

Socially responsible investing has grown to a point where it is not a fad. A significant number of people and institutions are investing their assets with an objective of both a financial return and a social return: the double bottom line. That said, there are several trends related to socially responsible investing that are worth mentioning.

One trend is the increasing number of investment options available to socially responsible investors. The very large mutual fund complexes now offer socially responsible mutual funds and many exchange traded funds (ETFs), which are both socially and responsibly oriented as well. Investment advisors are becoming more skilled at implementing socially responsible investment portfolios as well. This is another indication that socially responsible investing has now become mainstream. With the number of socially responsible investing alternatives, an investor most likely can find an investment or advisor that will implement a portfolio that closely meets their investment objectives.

As of the end of 2018, the Forum for Sustainable and Responsible Investment (USSIF) Foundation reported that socially responsible investments totaled $12 trillion compared to $8.7 trillion in 2016.[11] This equates

---

11. "2018 Report on US Sustainable, Responsible and Impact Investing Trends," the Forum for Sustainable and Responsible Investment, October 31, 2018, *https://www.ussif.org/trends*.

to a 38 percent increase. This increase demonstrates that socially responsible investing is now clearly mainstream, as evidenced by the following examples. A group of investors that include Bill and Melinda Gates formed a $2 billion green energy fund with a focus on reducing greenhouse gas emissions. Equally important, the United Nations has established a focus on responsible investing by sponsering the Principles of Responsible Investing. As of March 2019, over 1,900 asset managers with more than $81 trillion in assets have signed on to these principles.[12]

More and more investors are seeking to demonstrate their values with their investments to maximize their financial and social return. Younger investors appear to be particularly interested in socially responsible investing. A recent Morgan Stanley survey revealed that 8 in 10 millennials are interested in socially responsible investing.[13] Millennials are forecasted to increase their net worth to an amount estimated to range from $19 trillion to $24 trillion by 2020.[14] This could continue to increase socially responsible investing assets. Investors and investment advisors that ignore socially responsible investing do so at their own peril, as significant assets and resources are being invested in a socially responsible investing manner.

Socially responsible investors, as we have seen, have learned that they can have more impact by joining together in community. The Interfaith Center on Corporate Responsibility (ICCR) is one example. Numerous organizations have formed over the years around a specific purpose or issue. As an example, there is much current discussion on whether to include or exclude fossil fuel companies in investment portfolios. The trend of forming communities or organizations around environmental, social, or governance issues is likely to continue as younger investors are more focused on socially responsible investing. An investor committed to a particular issue and that wants to be engaged most likely can find an organization that shares their values.

---

12. "About the PRI," Principles for Responsible Investment, accessed April 1, 2019, *https://www.unpri.org/pri/about-the-pri*.

13. Millennials are broadly defined as those born between the early 1980s and 2000. See "Are Millennials Democratizing Sustainable Investing?" Morgan Stanley, March 6, 2017, *https://www.morganstanley.com/ideas/millennial-sustainable-investing*.

14. "Millennials and Wealth Management: Trends and Challenges of the New Clientele," Deloitte, accessed May 30, 2019, *https://www2.deloitte.com/content/dam/Deloitte/lu/Documents/financial-services/lu-millennials-wealth-management-trends-challenges-new-clientele-0106205.pdf*.

Multiple Voices

This book incorporates a unique collaboration of voices from multiple Christian denominations. Each denomination is encountering more and more of its members and institutions interested in socially responsible investing. While denominations may have varied tactics on implementing socially responsible investing, all denominations have faced opportunities and issues related to socially responsible investing. It is through sharing these opportunities and issues that each denomination can faithfully and better serve one another.

This book is attempting to do just that by sharing our denominations' experiences, perspectives, and resources. We all hope that this book will help church leaders to feel more informed on the issues and to be empowered for decisive action that reflects their Christian values through their investments.

Summary

There are many resources available that can assist investors in implementing socially responsible investment portfolios. While this book is intended to provide a solid base of understanding, it is not meant to prescribe the best, or a particular or preferred way to implement socially responsible investing.

The spectrum of socially responsible investors is broad. Some investors simply want to implement negative screens. Others may want to employ positive screens to include companies that have good policies and practices related to environmental, social, and governance (ESG) concerns. Still others might want to become more active shareholders through shareholder advocacy. Finally, those that are interested and able might want to go a step further and consider types of impact investing or community investing. Our hope is that this book will assist you in discerning the best approach for your congregation/organization. We greatly appreciate your interest and concern for these very important issues and your willingness to consider having your investments match your values.

Chapter 2

What This Means for My Congregation/Organization*

Greg Rousos

Introduction

Chapter 1 provided an introduction and definitions of investing basics and socially responsible investing. This chapter builds on that introduction and is intended to aid a church institution or congregation considering implementing an investment portfolio from a socially responsible perspective. This chapter might seem like a big jump from chapter 1. Please remember we have resources available in the appendix to further explain and provide examples of the concepts. Your denomination or denominational foundation is also an excellent resource if you find that you have questions or if additional information would be helpful.

This chapter uses an *investment policy statement* to guide the considerations of implementing an investment portfolio. An investment policy statement is the governing document that provides policy for an investment portfolio. The chapter closes with a discussion on socially responsible portfolio implementation considerations, fiduciary considerations, and available socially responsible funds and investments, as well as differing views locally, nationally, and internationally. If you are interested in socially responsible investing, our hope is that this chapter will help you start this exciting journey to align your investments with your values.

Socially Responsible Investing Considerations

Years ago, socially responsible investing was rarely talked about, and as a result, awareness was low. In addition, there were not many socially

---

* This material, including organizations and websites noted, is provided for informational purposes only and should not be viewed as an endorsement or as investment, tax, or other professional advice.

responsible investing options available for church institutions. Today, many people are aware of the general idea behind socially responsible investing. As noted in the previous chapter, millennials are particularly interested in socially responsible investing. If they have not already, a church institution's members may start asking their leaders if the funds are invested according to their values.

Leaders should prepare for questions regarding whether the church institution's assets are invested in a socially responsible manner. Colleges and universities are receiving questions and challenges from students who want to engage with university leadership regarding the investment of the university's endowment. Students today might focus on social justice and environmental issues and want to ensure that the university invests in line with those priorities. University leadership must be well versed in how the endowment is managed such that they can listen and respond to the students' questions appropriately. Similarly, leaders of church institutions should prepare for questions from their members regarding how the church institution's assets are invested.

The increasing awareness of socially responsible investing has led to more people being interested in socially responsible investing, which has resulted in an increased number of investment products and solutions. With the plethora of socially responsible investing alternatives, members and constituents may increasingly expect their church institutions to invest according to their values. Church institutions can look to their denomination's foundation, mutual fund complexes, and other investment advisors to find investment alternatives. With the increased number of products and providers, a church institution must consider and develop an investment policy statement to govern, both effectively and proactively, the investment portfolio of its assets.

Investment Policy Statement

The investment policy statement provides the policy and direction for investing the church institution's assets. The church institution should describe the investment goals and objectives in the investment policy statement with enough detail such that staff and investment advisors can implement the proper portfolio for the assets described in the investment policy statement. The board and investment committee of the organization should review and approve the investment policy statement at least annually.

An investment policy statement can be a lengthy and rather involved document. A church institution should not be deterred by the length or complexity. Instead, a church institution could consider developing the investment policy statement in steps. The investment policy statement is far too important of a document to neglect, and taking incremental action is a feasible way to draft and implement the policy.

Defining Investment Goals

The first step in determining how to invest a portfolio is for the investor to define their investment goals. The investment goals provide the high-level direction for the implementation and investment of the portfolio. The investment goals are a good introduction and guide the remainder of the investment policy statement.

The church institution should begin by determining the goals of the portfolio to be invested. For simplicity, we will discuss three types of portfolios: long-term, mid-term, and short-term.

Long-term portfolios are portfolios that are invested for greater than ten years. With this time period, long-term portfolios can accept more risk in the portfolio, which means a larger allocation to equity or stock securities. The objectives of long-term portfolios include capital appreciation or gains such that the portfolio grows to keep up with inflation and protect purchasing power. Diversification is important with long-term portfolios to provide exposure to multiple asset and sub-asset classes to manage risk and reduce volatility. Volatility is often the enemy of long-term portfolios, as volatile investment performance may not provide steady growth (especially for endowment/invested funds which provide regular distributions, as discussed below). A typical allocation for long-term portfolios is 60 to 70 percent in equity or stock securities and 40 to 30 percent in fixed income or bond securities. The portfolio must provide sufficient liquidity as needed to satisfy distribution requests.

A specific type of long-term portfolio is an endowment fund, which is often the focus of discussions on SRI. Endowment funds normally have principal restricted, where principal is to be held and invested for perpetuity. Endowment funds can either be classified as true endowment funds or quasi-endowments (also known as board-designated endowments). True endowments are funds where the *donor* restricted the assets in perpetuity. In other words, "principal" is not available for expenditure, but a conservative spending rate can be applied typically to an average value of the endowment over time. The organization can use that draw as the income from the true endowment, and those funds may have additional restrictions for specific purpose or use placed on them by the donor. Regarding quasi-endowment funds (board-designated endowments), since boards made these decisions on classifying these funds, future boards have the ability to change how they treat these funds. Therefore, quasi-endowment funds are expendable funds that the church institution treats "as if" they are permanent endowment funds, even though the original donor did not restrict principal or if the board chose to designate reserve funds or other unrestricted gifts to be treated "as if" they are true endowments, where the board takes an action to restrict principal from expenditure. Quasi-endowment funds can be spent beyond a conservative spending rate such that principal could be expendable (although this is not recommended for building faith and trust among future donors, see chapter 9). Many organizations invest their true and quasi-endowment funds together in the same investment allocation (strategy) but they track their different types of funds separately. Your investment advisors can often assist you with tools and methods for this.

Mid-term portfolios have a time horizon of three to ten years. Due to the shorter time period, mid-term portfolios should have less risk than long-term portfolios. This equates to a smaller allocation to equity or stock securities. Mid-term portfolios might have an asset allocation of 20 to 40 percent in equity or stock securities and the balance invested in fixed income and bond securities. Mid-term portfolios might include assets for capital expenditures and planned expenses, such as payouts for building expenses after funds for a capital campaign were raised.

Short-term portfolios have a time horizon of less than three years. Due to the shorter time horizon, the investor should limit or eliminate risk in this portfolio. Appropriate asset allocations for short-term portfolios include 0 to 20 percent in equity or stock allocation, 80 to 100 percent in fixed income or bond allocation, and the remaining allocation in cash. Examples of short-term portfolios include operating reserves and funds designated for operations or short-term projects. Operating reserve funds are critical to the organization. The church institution maintains operating reserve funds for daily operations and to manage through times of financial change or hardship. As such, the funds may be needed at any time. The protection of principal is of utmost importance for operating reserve funds, and the church institution should avoid investment risk with operating reserve funds.

The church institution should describe if any of these funds to be invested are unrestricted or restricted for specific purposes. An unrestricted fund allows the organization to use the fund however it deems best. Restricted funds are designated by the donor or board for a particular purpose or for a period of time. A restricted fund can be purpose-based, which dictates the way an organization must use the funds. A time-based restriction allows the organization to use the funds only when the time period is satisfied. Principal and income earned can be restricted by use or time. Spending from endowment funds, both "true" and "quasi," may have these additional restrictions toward specific purposes or programs or may be unrestricted to purpose. How funds are invested and spent can also have a direct impact on a donor's willingness to give additional gifts or inspire others to make a new gift (see chapter 9).

Investment Objectives

An investment policy statement should include an investment objective, as this will guide how the assets are invested and the types of securities in the portfolio. Investment objectives could include long-term capital growth, stable income, and safety, and the objectives are most likely guided by the investment goals of the portfolio.

Long-term capital growth describes a portfolio that is invested for the long-term that is focused on capital appreciation. As such, the portfolio will mostly invest in stocks or equity securities. This portfolio will experience realized and unrealized capital gains and losses. Stocks or equity securities offer lower income yields and they are considered a riskier asset class, though they typically have more potential for appreciation in value. Long-term portfolios have an investment objective that most closely aligns with long-term capital growth. Endowment funds are considered long-term portfolios and would have an investment objective of long-term capital growth.

An investment objective of *stable income* reflects a lesser focus on capital gains and an increased focus on yield or income derived from the investment. The investments that produce income are bonds and fixed income securities. These securities will not normally produce significant capital appreciation, but they will produce a more stable stream of income for the investor. Mid-term portfolios generally will have an investment objective of stable income with modest capital appreciation. Over time, as the mid-term portfolio's time horizon shortens, the stocks or equity holdings should be reinvested into bonds or fixed income. Funds for capital expenditure are normally considered mid-term funds and they would have an investment objective of stable income.

Safety reflects an investment objective where the investor wants to protect the value of the investment. The investor is willing to sacrifice capital appreciation and income to ensure the value of the investment does not decrease. Investments considered safe include government-issued bonds, certificates of deposits, and other cash equivalent investments such as money market funds. Operating reserve funds would be an example of short-term portfolios and would have an investment objective of safety.

Investment Considerations

The investment policy statement should include a discussion on considerations that can influence or dictate how the portfolios are invested. For a church institution, funds are governed by state law and the state attorney general. State law is an important consideration when constructing the investment policy statement. The Uniform Prudent Management of Institutional Funds Act (UPMIFA) provides specific guidance on charitable funds, particularly true (donor-designated) endowment funds. UPMIFA has been enacted in forty-nine states and the District of Columbia. As of this writing, Pennsylvania and Puerto Rico have not adopted UPMIFA.[1] UPMIFA includes provisions on true (donor-designated) endowment funds and their distribution policies. A church institution and its professional advisors should review UPMIFA to ensure the funds are managed in accordance with UPMIFA. However, UPMIFA also provides guidance on quasi-endowment funds, even if it does not legally govern them.

Another consideration in how portfolios are invested is the risk profile or risk tolerance of the church institution. The church institution should document their risk profile in the investment policy statement. There are many sources of risk profiles related to investments that are available to aid a church institution in understanding its risk profile. Investment advisors, denominational foundations, and certain websites have risk profiles that

---

1. "Understanding UPMIFA: Important Endowment Concepts," Planned Giving Design Center, accessed September 9, 2019, *https://www.pgdc.com/pgdc/understanding-upmifa-important-endowment-concepts.*

a church institution can use to develop its own risk profile. The risk profile should inform the church institution of how much investment risk the church institution is willing to accept. Church institutions that are more risk averse will have asset allocations that have higher allocations to bonds or fixed income securities and limit the amount of investment in riskier asset classes such as stocks or equity securities. An organization that is willing to accept risk will allocate more assets to stocks or equity securities.

Generally, church institutions do not need to consider tax consequences from their investments in most situations. However, a church institution that is not subject to corporate income tax might be subject to unrelated business income tax from certain investments, if they choose to invest in more complex asset classes or investments. Unrelated business income tax is generated when a church or non-profit realizes income from an activity not related to its exempt purpose. An example of unrelated business income is when a church institution invests in a partnership, like a hedge fund or private equity investment, which is debt financed. This specific, technical situation might give rise to unrelated business income tax according to the Internal Revenue Service. The church institution must make it clear in their investment policy statement if they are willing to invest in these vehicles and be subject to unrelated business income tax. If a charitable institution does realize unrelated business income, they may be required to file various forms with government agencies or other entities. A church institution should discuss whether they are willing to incur unrelated business income and consult appropriate professional legal or tax advice before making such investments. Your investment advisor can also often assist with these issues.

Distribution Policy

The distribution policy determines the amount of funds that are available for use by the church institution. A distribution policy is applicable for all portfolios; however, endowment funds (true and quasi) usually have more detailed and complex distribution policies. All portfolios should have a distribution policy to note when and how a church institution should receive and expend funds from the portfolio. For example, operating reserve funds might have a distribution policy that allows expenditures at times when there are financial operating deficits. Capital funds might have a distribution policy that allows for distributions when certain capital expenditures are incurred. As such, the investment policy statement should have a section for the distribution policy that makes it clear when and how a church institution may receive a distribution from the portfolio.

Distribution policies are particularly important for endowment funds due to their complex nature and investments. As discussed above, true endowment funds (as governed by UPMIFA in nearly every state) have the principal restricted for perpetuity based upon the principles of total return and prudent investment, with the spending restricted to purpose in some cases. Church leaders, attorneys, and accountants have had various definitions of net income or yield, although a common definition is interest and dividends less fees. Gains on securities are historically classified as principal.

Prior to UPMIFA and other predecessor laws and regulations, permanent endowment funds were invested typically in bonds or fixed income securities and dividend-producing stocks or equity securities. The objective was to produce the highest amount of net income (yield) with a lesser focus on the capital appreciation of principal; endowment funds' long-term performance suffered as a result. This led to the Uniform Management of Institutional Funds Act (UMIFA), which provides rules on the distributions from an endowment fund. The broadening definition of allowable distributions from a permanent endowment fund resulted in changes to the investments of the permanent endowment funds. Although no longer applicable, a significant aspect of UMIFA was that a church institution could expend from the permanent endowment fund a portion of the capital appreciation to protect purchasing power and keep pace with inflation, as long as withdrawals did not diminish the fund under its original "historic dollar value." UPMIFA changed the previous understanding of "historic dollar value" as long as true endowments conform to its various guidelines involving prudent investment and prudent spending from the endowment. Unfortunately, many church leaders may have lingering knowledge of these older ways for investing endowment funds, causing much confusion among parishioner and investment committee alike.

Even though many church institutions embraced UMIFA, market volatility and other issues led to the enactment of the Uniform Prudent Management of Institutional Funds Act (UPMIFA), primarily drafted in 2006. As previously noted, UPMIFA governs true endowment funds where the donor has permanently restricted those funds in this way. While board-designated or quasi-endowments are not governed by UPMIFA, many church institutions have wisely applied UPMIFA concepts to these funds to build donor confidence and simplify investment and distribution processes. UPMIFA included expanded direction on distribution policy and included the following considerations:

- the duration and preservation of the endowment fund;
- the purposes of the institution and the endowment fund;
- general economic conditions;
- the possible effects of inflation and deflation;
- the expected total return from income and the appreciation of the investments;
- other resources of the institution; and
- the investment policy of the institution.[2]

Said in another way, UPMIFA allows an organization to spend a portion of the capital appreciation along with the net income such that distributions increase with increases in the permanent endowment fund. This allows the permanent endowment funds to keep pace with inflation and thus protects purchasing power. The calculation formula of the distribution from an endowment fund is known as the *spending formula*.

A spending formula provides benefits to the church institution. The distributions from a portfolio that are based on a spending formula will not be as volatile as distributions that are based on net income. A spending formula also produces a predictable distribution from the portfolio, one that will not fluctuate over the year. This is very helpful to any church institution in its budgeting process.

A challenge for the organization is to define a spending formula that is equitable to current beneficiaries of the program and to the future beneficiaries of program. This is known as *generational equity*. A spending formula that distributes too much from a permanent endowment fund favors current beneficiaries to the detriment of future beneficiaries. Conversely, a spending formula that distributes not enough from a permanent endowment fund harms the current beneficiaries while favoring future beneficiaries. It is difficult if not impossible for a church institution to develop the perfect spending formula such that there is generational equity at all times. Therefore,

---

2. Uniform Prudent Management of Institutional Funds Act, drafted by the National Conference of Commissioners on Uniform State Laws, July 7–14, 2006, *https://www.uniformlaws.org/Higher Logic/System/DownloadDocumentFile.ashx?DocumentFileKey=d7b95667-ae72-0a3f-c293-cd8621a d1e44&forceDialog=0.*

the church institution should review the spending formula periodically and make adjustments as necessary.

There are various spending formulas in use today. A congregation/organization should examine spending formulas to determine the best formula for the institution and program. An example of a spending formula includes averaging the market value of a permanent endowment fund for a defined number of quarter-ends or year-ends and multiplying this average by a spending rate. A very common example of this spending formula is to average the ending balance of the last twelve quarters (three years) of the endowment fund market value and then multiply that by 4 percent. Another spending formula is taking a percentage of last year's distribution multiplied by inflation and adding this amount to the remaining percentage multiplied by the average of the permanent endowment fund's market value for a period of quarters multiplied by a spending rate. An example of this spending formula is taking 80 percent of the last year's distribution multiplied by inflation and adding 20 percent of the average of the last twelve quarters of the permanent endowment fund market value multiplied by 4 percent.

Typically spending rates average between 3 and 5 percent. UPMIFA considers 7 percent as an imprudently high spending rate.[3] The rate is a critical component of the spending formula. The rate should equal the total expected investment return of the portfolio less fees and less expected inflation. A spending rate that is too high will erode principal and therefore favor current beneficiaries while a spending rate that is too low will overly accumulate capital gains and favor future beneficiaries.

The church institution should set the spending rate carefully. Defining the proper spending formula based on the UPMIFA considerations noted above is complex and technical. A church institution may consider employing a consultant or someone with the requisite experience and technical expertise, such as their denomination's foundation staff or other investment professionals, to assist in determining the proper spending formula.

As mentioned above, all portfolios should have a defined distribution policy, whether they are short-term, mid-term, or long-term portfolios. The distribution policy informs how the portfolios are invested to ensure there is liquidity and appropriate growth to satisfy the distribution requirements of the portfolios.

---

3. Uniform Prudent Management of Institutional Funds Act, drafted by the National Conference of Commissioners on Uniform State Laws, July 7–14, 2006, accessed June 21, 2019, *https://www.uniform laws.org/HigherLogic/System/DownloadDocumentFile.ashx?DocumentFileKey=d7b95667-ae72-0a3f-c293-cd8 621a d1e44&forceDialog=0.*

Liquidity

The investment policy statement should include the liquidity needs of the portfolio. *Liquidity* is the ease of converting an asset to cash,[4] and is often considered as the amount of money required to be available for distribution from the portfolio. Liquidity needs are important to note in the investment policy statement, as they influence asset allocation. The investment policy statement should document the amount of money held in cash or in readily marketable securities such that they are available for making distributions to an entity.

An investor must understand the liquidity needs of the portfolio to make certain that money is available or liquid in the portfolio to satisfy distribution requirements. For example, consider a pension fund that distributes money monthly to pension beneficiaries. The investor must plan for the distributions and ensure the assets are held in securities that can be sold in a timely manner to satisfy the distributions. During the great recession of the late 2000s, some investors did not have enough liquidity for distributions due to the decrease in the market value of liquid investments. An investor must plan and invest in a manner to ensure they have liquidity to meet their distribution requirements.

Socially Responsible Investing

An investment policy statement should provide the church institution's objectives and approach to socially responsible investing. The church institution's denominational foundation or polity offices might have guidance and direction on socially responsible investing that can assist the congregation/organization in developing this portion of the investment policy statement. Coupled with denominational guidance, a congregation/organization can look to its core values to define socially responsible investing objectives. *Core values* are the foundational beliefs and convictions of the organization. Core values help to define model behavior and actions that guide the congregation/organization in its work. Sample core values could include respect for all people, an inclusive culture, care for the environment, valuing diversity, human health and wellness, integrity, and transparency.

The investor can use their core values and denominational information to define the positive and negative screens in the socially responsible

---

4. James Chen, "Liquidity," Investopedia, June 25, 2019, *https://www.investopedia.com/terms/l/liquidity.asp*.

investing portfolio. At various times socially responsible investors have included or excluded specific companies based on the company's activities. The investor might exclude a company for social rights or justice issues, such as in the example discussed in chapter 1 related to South Africa, where specific companies were identified to be excluded from a portfolio.

The church institution should document in the investment policy statement the sectors and any specific securities it wishes to include or exclude from the portfolio. Increasingly socially responsible investors are implementing portfolios with positive screens identifying the types of companies they wish to include in the portfolio. The positive screens are often referred to as environmental, social, and governance (ESG) investing and include investing in companies whose policies and practices align with the organization's values. Additionally, when investing in the options available through a denomination or its foundation, pooled funds are normally available and can incorporate SRI and ESG factors and options, which may satisfy a religious organization's goals. (See the appendix for a list of various denominational resources.)

A congregation/organization implementing socially responsible investing in its portfolio should understand it is never a perfect implementation and it will never perfectly match its core values. There are challenges to implementing socially responsible investing. Examples include companies that earn a small portion of their revenue from activities that the institution wishes to exclude from their portfolio. Even though the implementation is not perfect, it should not deter an organization from investing in accordance with its values (see chapter 3).

Advocacy is another consideration for a socially responsible investor. The investor should consider if they wish to be an active shareholder or passive shareholder. An active shareholder votes proxies or company resolutions and might wish to participate in annual shareholder meetings. A church institution may look to its denomination's foundation and other entities for information on how to vote proxies or company resolutions. There are resources available to assist with advocacy, such as proxy voting vendors that offer a service where they will vote proxies based on the organization's directions.

One further consideration of socially responsible investing is impact investing (see chapter 8). The organization should document in the investment policy statement if a portion of its portfolio is to be used for such activities. The organization might consider a percentage of its portfolio to allocate to impact investing. Again, denomination resources may provide impact investing opportunities. Options for community benefit, like revolving loans or other options, can have meaningful social impact even with a small allocation of the congregation/organization's portfolio.

Asset Allocation

A very important component of the investment policy statement is the asset allocation of the portfolio. Numerous studies have demonstrated that asset allocation is the single largest determinant of the portfolio's investment performance. The investment goals, objectives, risk tolerance, and other factors of the investment policy statement inform the asset allocation.

The asset allocation is as general or specific as the investor determines. At a high level, the asset allocation should document the percentage of the portfolio in stocks or equity securities, the percentage invested in bonds or fixed income, and the percentage held in cash. Long-term portfolios such as permanent endowment funds will have a greater allocation to stocks or equity securities while short-term portfolios will have a greater allocation to cash and bonds or fixed income securities.

Stocks, bonds, and cash are categories of asset classes. Asset classes are groups of securities with similar characteristics. Sub-asset classes break down asset classes into more categories. For example, the stock asset class could include subasset classes of large capitalization (large-cap), middle capitalization (mid-cap), and small capitalization (small-cap) companies, as well as further derivations for international, emerging market, US only, etc. The policy should include definitions of asset and sub-asset classes and target allocations for each sub-asset class and asset class. Along with the target allocations, the policy should include the upper and lower acceptable ranges for the allocations to the sub-asset and asset classes.

After defining the asset allocation, the church institution should consider the most efficient manner to implement the asset allocation. Investors with multiple millions of dollars to invest may consider purchasing individual stock and bond securities for the portfolio. However, in many instances, the use of pooled funds is most advantageous. The investor would need to identify pooled funds that match the asset allocation in the investment policy statement (IPS). Pooled funds offer the advantage of not having to select individual securities, providing diversification for even small investments, and automatically rebalance the investments among asset classes. Strategic asset allocation is an important concept that should be included in an IPS. While we will not discuss strategic asset allocation in this book, an institution should work with their investment advisor to understand the concept and the advisor's plans for this. Please seek the assistance of professional investment advisors, including your denominational resources or denominational foundation, on all of these topics. Most pooled funds do strategic allocation at a reasonable cost or operating expense. The investor should consider the portfolio's socially responsible investing objectives to see if the pooled fund matches those objectives. While the pooled fund will not allow the investor to vote proxies or file shareholder resolutions, a socially responsible pooled fund still allows an investor to demonstrate and live out their values through their investment.

Rebalancing

As previously noted, *rebalancing*, reallocating the proportion of your assets in particular types of investments, is an important consideration, as it can influence the portfolio's performance. Rebalancing allows the portfolio to stay consistent with the investment objectives and the asset allocation. The policy should document when the securities in the portfolio are to be traded to rebalance the portfolio such that it is in line with the asset allocation. The portfolio's asset allocation can become out of balance due to market performance and other factors. As an example, when the stock or equity markets outperform other markets, the portfolio becomes overweighted in stock or equity securities. Rebalancing between asset categories is needed to bring the portfolio in line with the strategic asset allocation targets.

An investor can rebalance the portfolio based on a time frequency, when there are defined deviations to the asset allocation target ranges, or when distributions are scheduled. Many church institutions choose to rebalance when there are distributions to be made to the entity since securities usually must be sold to meet the distribution requirements. The organization should consider selling securities in asset classes that are overweight to the asset allocation policy targets to rebalance the portfolio. Pooled funds composed of different asset and sub-asset classes will rebalance without the investor's intervention.

Portfolio Performance

An investment policy statement should include a goal or benchmark for investment performance. The investment performance goal should be reflected as a comparison to an industry benchmark. The industry benchmark can serve as a comparison to the actual performance of the portfolio. The industry benchmark should have a similar asset allocation to that of the portfolio. The comparison of the portfolio to an industry benchmark is important to ensure the portfolio is performing effectively. Most denominational foundations and other investment providers will use industry benchmarks, or an appropriately derived blended benchmark, to allow accurate comparisons to standard market performance.

Investment Policy Statement Responsibilities

The congregation/organization might engage several parties to manage the portfolio, including staff and board members. The investment policy statement should make clear each party's responsibility in managing the portfolio. For example, the board and investment committee are responsible for reviewing and approving the investment policy statement. Staff might be responsible for implementing the investment policy statement, or the investment committee might engage an investment advisor or consultant to implement the IPS.

It is important to note in the investment policy statement who oversees and monitors the performance of the investment advisor, staff, and the board and its investment committee. The board and investment committee should assess if they have the expertise and resources to carry out their responsibilities. If not, the board and committee should consider hiring staff or engaging consultants and firms with expertise to manage the organization's portfolios. Most denominational foundations can also help in these decisions.

Annual Review of the IPS

The investment policy statement is not a static document. The board and its investment committee should review and approve the investment policy statement at least annually. If your organization is fortunate enough to have the human resources for it, staff should review the IPS and the portfolio's performance more frequently and notify the investment committee of suggested changes.

The investment policy statement is the single most important document that governs the portfolios of the organization. An example investment policy statement is included in the appendix, and there are multiple examples available on the internet by simply searching. You can also contact your denomination's foundation or the other investment resources listed in this book's appendix for assistance with these documents. The board, investment committee, and staff must ensure that the investment policy statement accurately reflects the goals and objectives of the portfolios such that the portfolios are invested properly.

Socially Responsible Investing Implementation Considerations

The evolution of socially responsible investing makes this type of investing much more accessible to church institutions. There are several considerations a congregation/organization should evaluate prior to implementing a socially responsible portfolio.

As previously noted, the first consideration is the cost to operate a socially responsible investment portfolio. A socially responsible investment portfolio has more responsibilities than a standard portfolio. These responsibilities might include developing a list of companies or industries to screen either positively or negatively in the portfolio, researching and voting on company resolutions and the cost related to filing shareholder resolutions, and participating in annual shareholder meetings. These additional responsibilities may result in a socially responsible investing portfolio costing much more to invest and manage.

Another consideration is the investment performance of a socially responsible portfolio. Some might argue that a socially responsible portfolio should perform better than a standard portfolio over the long term since the socially responsible portfolio is investing in companies with good environmental, social, and governance policies and practices. However, if the socially responsible portfolio implements negative screens or excludes companies or sectors from potential investment, this limits the number of companies or sectors available for investment. Fewer investment options could limit the ability to diversify the portfolio. A portfolio that is less diversified could experience more risk and volatility. This could negatively (though sometimes positively as well due to the concentrations of certain assets in the portfolio) impact the portfolio's investment performance, particularly over shorter periods of time, especially if regular withdrawals would need to be taken in prolonged periods of underperformance. Over longer periods of time, socially responsible investments will have the ability to overcome short-term performance shortfalls. The additional costs, if any, of operating such a portfolio can also negatively impact investment performance.

Since socially responsible portfolios are customized to the investors' values, it might be difficult to evaluate their cost and performance compared to a standard portfolio or another socially responsible portfolio (see chapter 3). Portfolios might have different screens, costs, and investment options, which can create comparison challenges. It is even harder to compare the cost and performance of a socially responsible portfolio to a standard portfolio. The investor must first make the decision as to whether to invest in a socially responsible portfolio and then determine the best way to implement that portfolio based on their goals and objectives. Pooled funds that incorporate SRI and ESG factors available through denominational foundations or other financial institutions may make this process easier.

Fiduciary Considerations

One of the responsibilities of the board and investment committee of a congregation/organization is the proper management and oversight of the institution's assets, specifically its investable funds. This places the board and investment committee in a fiduciary capacity. A *fiduciary* is defined as "a person, company or association holding assets in trust for a beneficiary. The fiduciary is charged with the responsibility of investing the money wisely for the beneficiary's benefit."[5] A fiduciary has an important responsibility and must act in the best interest of the beneficiary. As such, board and investment committee members should not seek or attempt to gain personal benefit from their relationship with the church institution.

A fiduciary must ensure that funds are invested and used appropriately. The discussion above regarding developing an investment policy statement is the responsibility of the fiduciary. A fiduciary must comply with policy and the fiduciary must oversee and manage the parties responsible for implementing the investment policy statement. These parties could include staff and consultants hired to perform this work, as previously discussed.

---

5. John Downes and Jordan Elliot Goodman, *Barron's Dictionary of Finance and Investment Terms*, 4th ed. (Hauppauge, NY: Barrons Educational Series, 1995).

One place a fiduciary can look to for guidance is your state's UPMIFA or similar laws in your state (as of the writing of this book, the District of Columbia and forty-nine states except Pennsylvania have passed UPMIFA). UPMIFA requires that fiduciaries respect donor intent, act in good faith with the care of a prudent person, incur reasonable costs, diversify investments, and develop an investment strategy appropriate for the funds and church institution. The board or investment committee is also directed by UPMIFA to consider general economic conditions, inflation or deflation, tax consequences, expected total returns, and the needs of the church institution when determining investment policy and distribution policy.

An important responsibility of a fiduciary is to ensure that the funds are used in accordance with donor or board restrictions. If funds are restricted, the fiduciary must understand the restrictions and verify that the funds are used in accordance with the restriction. In recent years there are more cases of donors filing claims against a fiduciary and organization because the donors believe that the funds have not been used as designated by the donor.

A fiduciary is responsible for the prudent investment of the organization's funds. This includes diversifying the assets of the funds based on the fund's investment policy statement. If the fiduciary holds one or a limited number of securities in a portfolio, that may not be considered proper diversification. A portfolio that is not properly diversified could suffer from volatile or poor investment performance, as the performance of one security could overly influence the performance of the portfolio. Lack of diversification could give rise to claims against the fiduciary. The fiduciary should ensure that funds are properly diversified to minimize investment risk and the risk to the organization.

Reasonable costs are another important responsibility of the fiduciary. The fiduciary must ensure that the fees charged by investment advisors and other service providers are reasonable when compared to others.

The fiduciary must make certain that appropriate governance structures and resources are in place. Proper governance includes a board (or appropriate governing group as qualified for your denomination, e.g., vestry, etc.) and an investment committee to set and monitor policy. The investment committee performs the more detailed work of constructing the investment policy statement, providing oversight and managing investment advisors and staff, and reporting its work to the full board. The board should ensure there is appropriate expertise on the investment committee and should require diversity on both the investment committee and the board. The investment committee should have a charter that details its roles and responsibilities that the board approves. The board should review its governing documents, such as the articles of incorporation and bylaws, to verify it is operating in compliance with these documents.

Available Socially Responsible Funds and Investments

The growth of socially responsible investing has caused numerous mutual funds and investment advisors to develop and offer socially responsible investments. An investor can find socially responsible investing solutions at large and small mutual fund complexes and through registered investment advisors, as well as through denominational resources.

Mutual fund complexes offer a wide variety of socially responsible investing options. These options consist of negatively and positively screened mutual funds. An investor must review these options carefully to ensure the screens meet their objectives defined in the investment policy statement. The investor should review the actions related to advocacy to determine if the way the mutual fund votes proxies and files shareholder resolutions is consistent with their values and policy. Mutual funds and pooled funds are viable options for congregations/organizations, although they have little to no influence over a mutual fund regarding the socially responsible policies adopted and implemented.

There are investment advisors that will tailor a portfolio for the church institution that complies with their socially responsible investing objectives. While this might sound enticing, the organization should perform due diligence on the investment advisor to understand their performance track record and the fees charged against the portfolio. Typically, a customized portfolio will have higher fees than a mutual fund or standard portfolio.

Last and certainly not least, a congregation/organization should consider their denominational foundation or the various investment resources from its denomination. The denominational foundation normally will invest in accordance with the values and resolutions of the denomination, which most likely closely match the church institution's objectives. By investing and partnering with the denominational foundation, the church institution will benefit from the advocacy activities of the denominational foundation as well. An important benefit of investing with the denominational foundation is that fees earned by the denominational foundation are used to support the work of the denomination, which is not the case with fees paid to mutual funds and secular investment advisers.

Socially Responsible Investing Views

Local, national, and global views vary on socially responsible investing. While there are socially responsible investors around the world, their definition and application might differ. Church institutions in some countries are more strident with their implementation of socially responsible investing. In certain countries, church institutions will not consider the cost or the investment performance impact of a socially responsible portfolio and simply mandate that they implement a socially responsible portfolio. Denominations in the United States might be committed to socially responsible investing; however, their congregations and other institutions might not follow the denomination's lead for a variety of reasons.

Another difference relates to screening and the companies that are included or excluded from a portfolio. A congregation/organization's awareness or relationship with a local company can impact whether the church institution wants to include or exclude that company from their portfolio based on their knowledge of that company's work. As well, sectors that are screened for inclusion or exclusion from a portfolio can differ due to the country or state of the church institution. For example, some denominations in Europe will exclude a nuclear energy company or a company that exploits animals. That might not be the case for denominations in other parts of the world. Security screening can be different based on local, national, and international knowledge and perspectives.

Summary

This chapter built on the definitions and background of socially responsible investing in the first chapter and discussed the implementation and considerations of a socially responsible portfolio. There can be a lot to implementing a socially responsible portfolio. Please do not be deterred due to the effort involved. The best approach is to simply start by making incremental steps toward implementation. It is difficult and rare to find an investor that feels their socially responsible portfolio is perfect. Do not let a desire for perfection stop you from investing in accordance with your values. More of this is discussed in the chapter ahead with some exciting real-world examples and some helpful resources.

Chapter 3

Is Perfect the Enemy of the Good? Starting Socially Responsible Investing Incrementally*

Kathryn McCloskey

One of the Pharisees asked Jesus to eat with him, and he went into the Pharisee's house and took his place at the table. And a woman in the city, who was a sinner, having learned that he was eating in the Pharisee's house, brought an alabaster jar of ointment. She stood behind him at his feet, weeping, and began to bathe his feet with her tears and to dry them with her hair. Then she continued kissing his feet and anointing them with the ointment. Now when the Pharisee who had invited him saw it, he said to himself, "If this man were a prophet, he would have known who and what kind of woman this is who is touching him—that she is a sinner." Jesus spoke up and said to him, "Simon, I have something to say to you." "Teacher," he replied, "speak." "A certain creditor had two debtors; one owed five hundred denarii, and the other fifty. When they could not pay, he canceled the debts for both of them. Now which of them will love him more?" Simon answered, "I suppose the one for whom he canceled the greater debt." And Jesus said to him, "You have judged rightly." Then turning toward the woman, he said to Simon, "Do you see this woman? I entered your house; you gave me no water for my feet, but she has bathed my feet with her tears and dried them with her hair. You gave me no kiss, but from the time I came in she has not stopped kissing my feet. You did not anoint my head with oil, but she has anointed my feet with ointment. Therefore, I tell you, her sins, which were many, have been forgiven; hence she has shown great love. But the one to whom little is forgiven, loves little." Then he said to her, "Your sins are forgiven." But those who were at the table with him began to say among themselves, "Who is this who even forgives sins?" And he said to the woman, "Your faith has saved you; go in peace." (Luke 7:36–50)

The sinful woman of Luke's Gospel is not perfect. From the reading, one can surmise that she had a town-wide reputation. Simon's assumption—that

---

* This material, including organizations and websites noted, is provided for informational purposes only and should not be viewed as an endorsement or as investment, tax, or other professional advice.

Jesus Christ's allowance of her tearful ministrations was a signal that he was not an all-knowing prophet—prompts rebuke. In his words to Simon, Jesus Christ teaches us that her faithfulness, her service, and her constancy were far preferable to her having a "spotless record." Jesus's estimation of this woman, and forgiveness of her sins, shows us that it is far better to move toward faith and act accordingly than to achieve perfection.

In the Bible, we see again and again that ministry does not end with confronting sinners and demanding repentance. Prophetic witness welcomes transition, societal shifts, and redistribution of political might, and above all peaceful resolution and reconciliation of communities and associations with their moral calling and missions.

This witness advocates for the rightness of dialogue and resolution that extends beyond dispute, and into the toil of directly engaging with the people whom we would seek to persuade toward betterment. The Bible teaches us, through countless stories, including the sinful woman's, that the love of God is unbounded—and conversely, that God's love reaches to those with whom we disagree or deem incorrect. Refusal to "do what we can" to engage the other creates the black-and-white space that disavows compromise and steady work for good. Forgiveness, transformation, redemption, and growth are universal when we are called together to love our God.

So it should be with our congregations/organizations. What matters is service to the love of God, and not the achievement of purity. Whether through ministering to the homeless, the spiritual education of children, or the stewardship of financial resources, parishes must act with the goal of doing as much good in the world as possible. In doing so, churches and church entities should find their own voices in expressing commitment to the responsible use of financial resources. Congregations/organizations' ability to maximize the effectiveness of multiple, evolving strategies fosters mutual respect for the work of ministries' purpose, calling, and limitations. Amplifying the impact of cumulative strategies increases the probability of influencing social change and stepping nearer to God's intentions for humankind and Creation.

United Church Funds is an associated ministry of the United Church of Christ, investing on behalf of churches and institutions of the UCC, with the vision of "Investment that creates a just world for all."[1] We have been an integral part of many churches' journeys toward financial resource stewardship in a faith-aligned manner. This process has not always been as

---

1. "Mission, Vision & Values," United Church Funds, accessed July 21, 2019, *https://ucfunds.org/mission-vision-values/*.

linear as a church endowment committee easily deciding to invest its assets in a responsible manner and then instructing United Church Funds to act as their financial partner. There have been decades of vision and revision of what it means to be a good (and not perfect) faith-based investor. As with many denominations, the United Church of Christ began its responsible investing debates with the onset of the knowledge of apartheid in South Africa and a desire to assist, or the desire to have clean hands, depending on the party. First in 1969, and then many times subsequently, the United Church of Christ issued responsible investing suggestions to its churches, entities, and members through its national assembly, the General Synod. The 1969 General Synod affirmed its Council on Financial Investments position, which indicated that responsible investing is an appropriate method for a church-related institution to marry mission with assets: "All Instrumentalities and Conferences should actively seek involvement consistent with General Synod policies to achieve socially beneficial change in corporate practice through their ownership of financial instruments."[2]

Many settings of the United Church of Christ continue to use the Council on Financial Investments' position—and other General Synod resolutions—as the baseline premise with which to create ethical guidelines. The evolution of the policies that govern United Church Funds' responsible investing has been gradual. At one point, UCF didn't even have a statement of its policies, but now has several codified expressions of its faith-based investing. These have undergone periodic changes—responding to the times and to the changing realities of investing as well as to the changing moral code of the denomination UCF serves. Of course, this is appropriate. If UCF had left stagnant its responsible investing strategies, it wouldn't accurately represent the will of its clients any longer. Nor would those strategies even cover all of UCF assets—the instruments and places that UCF invests have grown and changed over time. For example, United Church Funds has included the following language in its investment policy statement:

> United Church Funds' efforts toward fostering a just and sustainable economic system and world include several effective strategies. Exclusionary screening is just one practice that examines the Environmental, Social, and Governance (ESG) impacts of the corporations in which we have invested. ESG considerations have always been a moral and performance issue for UCF, and the

2. United Church Funds, Inc., and The Pension Boards—United Church of Christ, Inc., "Resolution Urging Socially Responsible Investment Practices: A Resolution of Witness," accessed June 17, 2019, *http://uccfiles.com/pdf/16-RESOLUTION-URGING-SOCIALLY-RESPONSIBLE-INVESTMENT-PRACTICES.pdf.*

wider investing industry now increasingly acknowledges the importance of ESG factors. In addition to exclusionary screening, United Church Funds utilizes shareholder advocacy, investor statements on public policy and regulations, and intentional proxy voting on behalf of the United Church of Christ's assets. In an effort to drive positive outcomes, United Church Funds also seeks opportunities in impact investing. United Church Funds endeavors to be a faithful representative of the principles of the United Church of Christ in its responsible investing program, but will always maintain the proper fiduciary controls over the assets entrusted to us. United Church Funds exclusionary screens reflect what is feasible and relevant for the Still Speaking faith.[3]

There is nuance in the language above. We seek faith consistency; we also maintain fiduciary control. We believe that investing can be transformative to certain social and environmental problems, but we don't seek purity. United Church Funds' clients understand this duality and understand the need for holding several concepts in balance.

How can a congregation/organization begin the process of finding their path toward responsible investing? What are the building blocks of sound responsible investing policies? How can a congregation/organization find effective partners? How does it keep moving without fearing for "getting it all right"?

Begin Where the Church Is

Whether or how to invest responsibly does not begin in a meeting of the church's endowment committee. It is a whole church decision. What is the mission of the church? What are the social issues that define the parish? What are the demographics of the congregation and of the surrounding community? These questions are imperative to decipher and determine next steps.

For example, a church starting an endowment for the first time may have very different needs than a well-endowed church, and that may mean that the social responsibility aims of the new endowment may be very different. It is less likely that a church beginning its endowment will be able to invest in cutting-edge environmental solutions funds, and most likely will consider mutual funds (or "commingled" pooled funds) as a first step. The whole church should be given the opportunity to accept this as forward momentum toward the parish's ultimate goals, and the endowment committee should be

---

3. "Statement of Investment Policy," United Church Funds, October 2017, *https://ucfunds.org/wp-content/uploads/2018/01/UCF-Statement-of-Investment-Policy_FINAL2017.pdf.*

prepared to hold periodic discussions with the congregation and its leaders around aligning values to mission as the endowment grows. Reevaluating the mutual funds in which it's invested should be a critical part of the church's responsibility. The more the church can integrate discussions of its mutual funds' investment performance with social and environmental performance, the better evaluative tool the church will have when determining whether to make a change to its financial partner or mutual fund provider.

In another example, consider a church that has a modest endowment that has been invested with the local investment broker for a very long time. It is appropriate for this church to begin by asking the right questions: Are there ways that the current broker can direct their assets in a way that will have the same return profile with a superior ESG profile? What would those costs be? If the church receives information indicating that it is impossible to line up long-term ESG goals with the investments, then it is time to examine the next step of seeking a different investment opportunity, as current understanding of fiduciary duty is quite clear that both can be accomplished simultaneously.[4]

Know What the Church Says It Does

The most important communication regarding asset stewardship, both internal to the church family and external to a church's financial partner/s, is the investment policy statement. Each congregation/organization requires an investment policy statement—a public plan that describes how the endowment will be invested so that its assets will enable important ministries to continue (see chapter 2). In establishing a policy, a congregation/organization must identify investment goals—and connect expectations for growth, income, stability, return, and/or social responsibility. The policy should also consider risk tolerance, realizing that higher returns are generally understood to require greater risk. The policy will outline appropriate investment types and management resources. Importantly, the investment policy must set reasonable expectations based on investment choices.

As such, this document should be a place where socially responsible investing choices are recorded and decided following much discussion. Bright lines of "must have" aspects of responsible investing as well as when there is the moral space for gray area and flexibility should be delineated.

---

4. "Fiduciary Duty in the 21st Century," Fiduciary Duty, accessed April 22, 2019, *https://www.fiduciary duty21.org/english.html*.

Assets that may need exceptions to the SRI choices should be discussed as well. This perfect/good dynamic is never more imperative to discern than in the decisions above. Again, it's important to be aware that the vast majority of churches are involved in various pooled funds like mutual funds, or pooled funds and options offered through their denomination's foundation. Sometimes the socially responsible investing imperatives of your church don't line up one-to-one with the way mutual funds invest. Getting comfortable with a certain amount of flexibility is an important part of the work of the church at this point. For example, United Church Funds uses mutual funds to access particular asset classes when it would be prohibitively expensive to be in a separate account. When doing so, UCF commits that it will monitor the holdings of these mutual funds. When a fund's overall holdings consist of less than 2 percent of companies that UCF would otherwise eliminate for social reasons, the mutual fund is considered to be consistent with our socially responsible investing policies. When a fund's holdings consist of more than 2 percent of companies that UCF eliminates, it would be considered inconsistent and a conversation of its investment committee would determine next steps. Your institution's or denomination's parameters may be different.

Know If the Church Is Doing What It Says It Does

Once an investment policy is set, there is the business of sleuthing out where the investments currently lie. The example of a church with long-standing investments with a local broker is a scenario that the business development team at United Church Funds sees very often. It's comfortable, there are personal connections, and the broker is frequently a trusted member of the church. For many churches, that's a fine way to steward their assets.

For those congregations/organizations contemplating faith-aligning their assets, though, an accurate understanding of what the broker, or any intermediary, has done with the endowment so far is critical. Most likely a church is invested in funds consisting of a mix of stocks and bonds according to their risk/return expectations. Add the curveball of faith alliance, and some brokers/managers are flummoxed. Don't forget, too, that it is sometimes uncomfortable to be critical of the neighbor or fellow parishioner who is stewarding the church's money. It's a very real concern that a church may neglect its duties to its endowment so as not to upset the local broker. Every church should prioritize an examination of these types of relationships, not just for socially responsible investing aims, but also to conform to best practices and fiduciary standards. Normally having an outside professional investment advisor, like your denomination's foundation or other secular options, is best.

It is then that the congregation/organization must take on the job of evaluation. Here are the main questions they need to answer:

- Are we executing on the basics?
  - One of the fiduciary responsibilities of investment managers is to vote the ballots of the annual meetings of their invested stocks.
  - These voting rights of shareholders are an important way for investors to signal assent or dissent with corporate management policies and practices.
  - Proxy voting according to one's values is possible in certain situations.

While some proxy voting is mundane—voting to approve the audit report, electing longstanding board members—it is a crucial tool for communication. The ballot is one way to seek greater diversity in leadership; support shareholder resolutions calling for environmental, social, or governance improvements; and protest the elections of board directors that have overseen troubling practices. It is unlikely that a congregation/organization will be able to vote their own proxies, as they will most likely be investing in mutual funds, or other pooled vehicles previously discussed. As such, the question of how the mutual fund is voting proxies should be posed to the investment manager on a revolving basis.

A congregation/organization's financial partner should be able to describe their proxy voting policies and their resulting votes. These conversations are important icebreakers to some of the more difficult conversations regarding socially responsible investing. If it is determined that the financial partner is not voting according to the church's wishes, there are "off the shelf" responsible investing voting policies available through third-party vendors. The church leaders could encourage their financial partner to look into these options, if possible.

- Do we have current investments in industries or practices that are antithetical to our morals?
  - Unless the congregation/organization's investment policy statement dictates otherwise, it is fair to assume that the church is invested in industries or "sectors" that somewhat mirror an index like the Standard & Poor's 500. When an investment policy statement does

define those industries that are "out of bounds" for investment, this policy is known as exclusionary screening.

- ○ Choosing not to buy particular stocks or avoiding selected industries is the most widely practiced element of exclusionary screening.[5]

- ○ Many practitioners use revenue thresholds when possible to determine whether a company is significantly involved in a particular industry and should therefore be excluded. Setting the threshold is a critical step in our very global economy marked by conglomerates.

- ○ The outcome of revenue thresholds is that it is possible that an investment may still have exposure to the offending industry.

Here is another liminal space that the church must occupy. Even in this seemingly black-and-white decision of screening out X industry, there is gray area. There is the knowledge that present-day corporations are exceedingly complicated, with extensive supply chains and downstream operations that may include traces of the screened-out industry. Comfort with this imperfection will allow the balance of financial security or growth with the moral leanings of the church.

The knowledge of this complexity leads many SRI practitioners to set revenue thresholds. For example, United Church Funds' exclusionary screening policy prevents investment in a company that makes more than 10 percent of its annual revenue from the production of conventional weapons supplied to the US military. Setting this threshold allows investments in companies with meaningful business lines that are unrelated to weapons products—and limits those companies who for all intents and purposes are only weapons companies. This allowance assists in the diversification needs of modern investors.

Exclusionary screening policies should not be set-it-and-forget-it. What was once the moral understanding of the church may change and be shaped as society changes. In 2017, United Church Funds examined its exclusionary screens and made some changes—based on the teachings of the UCC's General Synod. The compelling screens of the 1970s to 1990s were mostly of a temperance model that sought to limit profit from the vices of alcohol, tobacco, and gambling. We found that our clients and our denomination had recently become less concerned with vice control and more energized by justice—such as the impropriety of deriving profit from private prison companies and companies

---

5. "Report on US Sustainable, Responsible and Impact Investing Trends 2018," Forum for Sustainable and Responsible Investing, accessed April 22, 2019, *https://www.ussif.org/files/Trends/Trends%202018%20 executive%20summary%20FINAL.pdf.*

with poor human rights records—and adapted our exclusionary screening policy accordingly. To do so, we gathered representative stakeholders of our clients and created a task force. In the church setting, these types of changes should be done in consultation with a wide group of members, not just within the endowment committee, and should be done with the knowledge that the church's expression of these changes may be limited by the funds available to them, as pooled funds will not be able to accommodate all restrictions.

- Do we believe that our investment partners should be using our assets to seek corporate change?

  o Corporate engagement is the process of seeking environmental, social, or governance improvements from invested assets.

  o Faith-based investors have a long history of seeking corporate improvements.[6]

  o ESG investors seek corporate improvements to better long-term performance expectations.

  o The engagement strategies of both faith-based and ESG investors are time-consuming but lead to trajectories of better-aligned investments for long-term investment health.

Depending on the church, there may be an expectation for or comfortability with the concept of activism for driving social change. Many faith-based institutional investors bring this action orientation into their investments. Such investors believe that there is the ability to drive improvements by the "insider approach" of being a shareholder. Through shareholder resolutions and dialogue, faith-based investors have been seeking change for decades.

Corporate engagement requires patient capital. Engagements may take several years to bear meaningful change. In addition, corporate engagement is less successful without the "outsider strategies" of legislative scrutiny, public outcry, and organized pushback. Churches seeking to be a part of greater movements would be likely candidates for corporate engagement–style investment management.

Lest we forget, the corporate engagement space contains the multitudes of perfection versus good enough. Some believe that waiting for corporate change on particular issues is not satisfactory. Particularly regarding environmental impacts, there are stakeholders that believe that incremental change

---

6. "History of ICCR," Interfaith Center on Corporate Responsibility, accessed April 22, 2019, *https://www.iccr.org/about-iccr/history-iccr*.

will not be enough to stem the deleterious effects of climate change in time. While practitioners have different views on this, it is the continued conversation that has allowed the investing space to come as far as it has with regard to climate sensitivity.

For a church, the most accessible way to prioritize shareholder engagement is to use an investment partner that does so on behalf of its clients. Selecting an investment manager that is committed to corporate change through the power of share ownership is one way a church can further its social and environmental priorities.

- Should our investment partners use environmental, social, and governance (ESG) markers to make investment decisions?

  ○ Investment managers increasingly believe that material (financially meaningful) ESG factors should be given consideration when examining the fundamental worthiness of a particular company.

  ○ Certain types of investors are more suited to an ESG style than others. A fundamental manager (stock picker based on insights) can more easily incorporate ESG markers into their investment process than a quantitative manager (uses financial data to make investment decisions).

  ○ There is an increasing number of investment management options for those that believe that ESG is relevant to performance.

With the knowledge that there is no such thing as a "pure" investment, it's important for investment managers to be able to describe what they see as the material ESG factors for an industry or sector. For example, the agriculture sector has high risks in water usage and labor rights issues but not data security. In a less encouraging example, a solar energy company may be part of the solution for long-term energy needs but may also have large polluting impacts on local waterways. The process, and determination of how to use these informational inputs, is what separates a manager with a real ESG focus from those paying lip service to the concept.

A congregation/organization considering ESG investment managers should know that there is sometimes a premium associated with this style. Fees may be higher than with traditional managers. For this reason alone, congregations/organizations should carefully weigh their comfort levels with the ESG process. Without a clear sense of the manager's ability to use these markers wisely, it may not be worth higher fees.

- Does our church benefit from our investment manager's involvement in investor partnerships?
  - There are many opportunities for investment managers and other financial intermediaries to signal their support for the ESG industry. The most prominent membership for an investment manager is the UN Principles for Responsible Investment as a signatory.
  - Many faith-based investors convene around the Interfaith Center on Corporate Responsibility.
  - Other issue-specific partnerships and coalitions are another way for investors to be involved.

One marker of a committed responsible investment manager is their ability to partner with like-minded firms for common outcomes. Working together allows assets to be pooled and influence to be amplified for change, such as being a signatory to the UNPRI.

The UN Principles for Responsible Investment are as follows:

- Principle 1: We will incorporate ESG issues into investment analysis and decision-making processes.
- Principle 2: We will be active owners and incorporate ESG issues into our ownership policies and practices.
- Principle 3: We will seek appropriate disclosure on ESG issues by the entities in which we invest.
- Principle 4: We will promote acceptance and implementation of the Principles within the investment industry.
- Principle 5: We will work together to enhance our effectiveness in implementing the Principles.
- Principle 6: We will each report on our activities and progress towards implementing the Principles.[7]

UNPRI signatories are annually assessed for how well they have grown with and lived into these principles. Parts of these assessments are publicly available. A congregation/organization can determine whether their investment managers have signed on to the UNPRI. As in all things, the UNPRI is not perfect. There are signatories that have done very little work on aligning

---

7. "What Are the Principles for Responsible Investment?" Principles for Responsible Investment, accessed April 22, 2019, *https://www.unpri.org/pri/what-are-the-principles-for-responsible-investment*.

their portfolios to ESG strategies. However, the "good" in the UNPRI is the groundswell of attention that is paid to the UNPRI, the communication among members that helps open minds to the concepts of ESG investing, and the "managing up" that the vanguard responsible investors have been able to accomplish with the biggest firms in the world.

In 2018, a large investment firm's CEO issued an open letter to the CEOs of its invested corporations. The letter informed the CEOs that it was time for them to start accounting for their corporations' societal impacts. The enormity of this sentiment, that the investment firm would begin to differentiate between those who accounted for their impacts and those who wouldn't, sent shock waves through the ESG investing world. Without the company's membership in, and view of the growth, of the UNPRI, it's possible that this letter would never have been written.

For churches, it may be less compelling that a large firm warns its invested companies to do better than it is to learn about what faith-based investors are doing in the areas of human rights and Creation care. These investors use a moral viewpoint for their actions, without discouraging the ESG impacts their actions may have. Faith-based investors are versed in reacting to a harm in a community or ecology and responding with insistent but care-filled urges for corporations to change. Arguably, the modern-day ESG movement is built on the work of faith-based investors. From a church's perspective, there are myriad memberships and subscriptions and sign-on opportunities for their financial partners. What's important is the ability of a firm to signal its intent through its partnerships and its follow-through on its aims.

- Do our investment managers and financial intermediaries prioritize diversity?

  - Research shows that gender diversity within the oversight of corporate firms is a predictor for more consistent returns (see chapter 5).[8]

  - Investing in minority-owned investment firms supports leadership and promotes more distinctive thinking.

- The previously mentioned letter also stated that the companies in which it invests should have at least two female directors. Another firm has asked companies to disclose their efforts to improve board diversity. And the New York State Common Retirement Fund indicated that it opposes the reelection of directors on US corporate boards that lack women.

---

8. Corinne Post and Kris Byron, "Women on Boards and Firm Financial Performance: A Meta-Analysis," *Academy of Management Journal* 58, no. 5 (November 7, 2014): *http://amj.aom.org/content/58/5/1546.abstract.*

The large investor concern in diversity arises from research that shows correlation between more women on boards with stronger, long-term financial performance. Studies from consultants, banks, and investment research firms bear out the correlations.[9]

Several years ago, United Church Funds had the opportunity to observe while a metropolitan, well-endowed church searched for a new investment consultant (see the case study on The Riverside Church, NYC). Throughout the process, this church was clear that racial diversity within their consulting team was an imperative. But their commitment didn't end there: each potential consultant was asked to bring its best ideas of how to incorporate minority-owned, emerging (less than $200M in assets) investment managers into their lineup. Those conversations weren't always easy, but the church was insistent that their consultant be able to identify these managers. In the end, this church may not have felt that a perfect solution was evident in one consultant. Instead, they created a novel response: they hired a traditional consultant to manage the bulk of their assets with a diverse team and hired a lesser-known advisor for sourcing emerging managers.

Not every church is well endowed and not every church can afford one investment consultant, let alone two. But these conversations, even if they don't ultimately yield changes to a church's investments, are incredibly instructive to the investing community. When clients indicate that they desire change, financial partners listen. Pressure to diversify staff and leadership, even from church clients, will continue the trend.

- Is our well-endowed congregation/organization capable of using our assets in a way that deepens our good in the world?

  - Impact investing is a new term for the concept of intentionally investing in finance vehicles designed to solve for environmental or social issues (see chapter 8).

  - Many impact investment opportunities focus on long-term investments rather than stocks and bonds that can be liquidated quickly.

  - Impact investing has the least amount of consensus among practitioners about measurements and return expectations.

  - While there are innovative and complicated impact investing vehicles designed for large amounts of capital, smaller congregations/

---

9. Credit Suisse, accessed April 22, 2019, *https://www.credit-suisse.com/about-us-news/en/articles/news-and-expertise/cs-gender-3000-report-2019-201910.html*; "The Tipping Point—Women on Boards and Financial Performance," MSCI, accessed April 22, 2019, *https://www.msci.com/www/research-paper/the-tipping-point-women-on/0538947986.*

organizations are able to access impact investing through community banks, credit unions, and similar structures.

A church that is comfortably endowed and has all of its short-term needs and rainy-day contingencies covered by its current investing strategies may consider the ability to dedicate part of its investments in higher social or environmental return vehicles. The number of qualifiers in the previous sentence may be noted—many of these investments are long-term in a way that a church reliant on its periodic financial inputs would probably eschew. The seeming imperfection of being separated from one's assets for a long time has a benevolent side effect, though: long-term capital to underbanked or traditionally overlooked parts of the economy takes time and does the most good with longer time horizons.

For a time, faith-based investors were solely seeking impact from asset classes like microfinance or community development financial institutions, which directed capital to people in the developing world or stateside that had little access to credit. These asset classes sought little return and created opportunities for entrepreneurs to make small incursions into business.

Now, the term "impact investing" encompasses myriad ideas: seeking both environmental and social solutions; in public markets and private; and in equity, debt, and alternative structures. For the congregation/organization considering investing with impact, it is very important to dig deep into the details: does their financial partner understand the social issue that they're trying to solve for in a way that is congruent with their understanding of the issue? Do the stated measures of success for the social issue seem to logically follow? Is the manager able to show how their measures of success map to industry-wide accepted standards like the GIIRS (Global Impact Investing Ratings System) or IRIS (Impact Reporting and Investment Standards)?

For the smaller church, the building blocks of impact investing are still accessible. Using a credit union for the church's banking needs is a great way to support egalitarian endeavors to serve members above maximizing profits. This nonprofit cooperative structure often prioritizes underserved segments of society for financial outreach and education. Similarly, community development loan funds are a way to invest in local communities and a time-tested way for churches to give back through their investment program.

- Does our congregation/organization receive enough information and communication from our financial partner about our social responsibility goals?

- From the congregation/organization's first inklings of desiring socially responsible investing through its maturation of the program, communication with all stakeholders is paramount.
- An annual conversation with the financial partner focused on social responsibility is a good start.
- What matters most is betterment over time from a congregation/organization's financial partner, and that thoughtfulness on social and environmental issues is allowed into the investment process.

There still exist financial partners that say that responsible or ESG investing can't be accomplished without sacrificing returns. A congregation/organization considering responsible investing should resist this flawed logic by "calling the question" insistently and unwaveringly. Through intentionally crafting the investment policy statement, whole-institution conversations together with the financial partners can demonstrate the environmental and social concerns of the congregation/organization and through regular check-ins demonstrate how financial partners are evolving in this space.

The congregation/organization that's called to use its voice in many ways to do God's work of transforming the world should consider responsible investing, and not be concerned with achieving the perfect plan immediately. Socially responsible investing offers a recognized and internationally legislated way to call for change while respecting the resource stewardship. Congregations/organizations that have not explored or accessed the benefits of socially responsible investing practices to join this movement and commit to transformation can do so gradually and methodically.

Congregations/organizations should consider socially responsible investing as an adjunct strategy alongside activism, intentional purchasing decisions, legislative improvements, awareness raising, and prayer. All settings of the church universal's witness of faith demonstrate the beliefs of justice to which all believers are called.

The choice to introduce a socially responsible investing program is not appropriate as a standalone strategy and is as subject to successes and failures as other acts of witness that speak truth to power. Finding a comfort level with the successes and failures is part of the struggle and should be embraced as much as possible. Create a path by holding love for those working with the church and work toward the best outcomes for the endowment and the long-term health of your parish, without falling prey to the false promise of perfection.

Chapter 4

Repairing the World One Company at a Time–Shareholder Advocacy*

*Byrd Bonner***

When we venture into new territory in the work of a local congregation or organization, we often feel as if we are the first or only ones to be doing that work. Whether it is feeding the homeless or organizing a youth group, the tendency can be to feel as if we are alone. That feeling can also be true for financial and investment management. For example, almost twenty years ago I staffed the launching of a planned giving program for a then-brand-new foundation. No one had ever been asked to make estate or planned gifts to some of the ministries to be benefited. I felt as if I was the only one with that challenge. Little by little I discovered many resources and advisors that would help me to build the program, just as they had built their own years earlier. As it turned out, I was not alone. Through the ecumenical and interfaith community, I found a team of colleagues that offered advice and guidance. It was up to me to find my way for my organization, but their support was irreplaceable.

In this chapter we will examine the "how-to" of starting a viable and sustainable "shareholder advocacy" program from scratch. My definition of that term is very broad in scope. It includes formal engagement through resolutions filed with publicly traded corporations, proxy voting, and more informal dialogues. It can take the form of letters of inquiry or concern, but more often takes on a more formal format, often including the opportunity to coalesce with other nonprofit groups with similar concerns. We will examine opportunities to lead a process within a congregation or faith-based organization to *repair the world* one company at a time. I have developed what

---

* This material, including organizations and websites noted, is provided for informational purposes only and should not be viewed as an endorsement or as investment, tax, or other professional advice.

** Editor's note: Although most congregations/organizations will not invest their endowment or invested funds to own stocks directly, some might; others may designate a portion of their assets to this purpose for a variety of reasons, such as a donor who may be interested in sponsoring such work (see chapter 9).

I refer to as the 4 Es: empower, engage, educate, encourage. By following these phases expanded upon in this chapter, you should be able to create a program that will become a source of pride and perhaps evangelism within your circle. As will be evident in this chapter, even though only direct shareholders can actually file shareholder resolutions (proposals submitted addressing a particular issue for vote at an annual meeting) and most congregations and entities do not or cannot hold individual shares among their invested assets, your denominational foundation and other entities through pooled funds and other investment vehicles are taking proactive action with respect to a number of issues that will be of great importance to your congregation/organization. This chapter is intended to inform and inspire all its readers on the processes involved, even if they cannot engage in all of the activities described.

Empower

The first step to begin a ministry or effort in social advocacy and responsible investment is to look around and map the assets that lie within the congregation or organization to assist you. Use this opportunity to gather information within your fiduciary committee (this may have a different name in your denomination) and congregation about experience with shareholder engagement such as proxy voting, dialogues with management, and shareholder resolutions. This collecting of information can take the form of informal conversations at the coffee urn or more formal written templates, e-mails, or web-based surveys. This process of information gathering from the congregation or constituents will also assist with the education process to be discussed later.

It is vital to have some guided conversation, perhaps an entire meeting's agenda, devoted to the role, duties, and outcomes for your committee. In whatever form it takes in your tradition, as the committee with responsibility for financial investment and impact of assets of your organization or congregation, you have special fiduciary duties that should be carefully discussed and defined. Just the mention of the word "fiduciary" in religious circles sometimes sends shivers up even the most seasoned spine! It is interesting if not puzzling since most of the relationships we engage in within the religious community are, indeed, fiduciary ones in some respect. The word "fiduciary" derives from the Latin *fiducia*. At its most common and basic definition, it simply means "trust." A fiduciary relationship or duty is one based on trust that one party or group places in another. When you think about it, most confirmation classes, lectionary groups, catechism or study groups, and certainly worship or *Shabbat* services are grounded in the trust placed in a teacher, preacher, rabbi, or group leader.

Our society has most often turned this duty of trust into one confined to the caretaking of money or financial sustainability. In fact, very often in the pension and retirement fund industry, the term "fiduciary committee" takes on a very specific role in the management of current funding to a future liability. I do not use the term "fiduciary committee" in so strict a sense. I will refer to the finance, investment, or endowment committee that has a duty to care for not only the investment of funds that have been entrusted to it, but also to care for the vision of ministry cast by the individual stewards who gave those funds to change lives and to repair the world. The preparation for the roles and responsibilities of a fiduciary committee for financial matters is beyond the scope of this chapter and book. Several firms and organizations offer excellent resources for financial oversight and investment processes.

Tools helpful to your ongoing process will include a good charter document for your committee that clarifies the deliverables for your work, to include faith-based screening and shareholder advocacy. The features of a committee charter may already be contained in your congregation/entity's bylaws or possibly your denomination's "book of order" or similar guideline documents within your own tradition. The charter should be submitted for approval to the body to which your committee is accountable, such as a board of directors or church council. Next, you will need a good investment policy statement (IPS) to guide your process (see chapters 2 and 3). In addition to the normal features of an IPS such as investment objectives, personnel—both lay and professional—asset allocation, and prohibited and allowable holdings, your policy should include your social advocacy objectives and strategies. This would include any social screens of industries or sectors that you do not want to own because of your theological or religious stances, noting a percentage of revenue to a company for those offending industries, as has been previously discussed. Examples might be companies that own or manage private prison facilities, companies that manufacture or market alcoholic beverages or tobacco products, or companies dealing in pornography. In addition, a commitment to or an allowance for shareholder advocacy and engagement is needed for the work covered in this chapter. While the priorities discussed later can be included in the IPS, it may be more prudent to state them, as well as guidelines on company revenue percentages for those aspects, in a separate approved policy so as not to require the amendment of your IPS each time you adjust your shareholder advocacy priorities.

The next step is to look outside of your congregation or organization for local, regional, or national coalitions and centers that already work in the field of faith-based investment and particularly shareholder engagement.

As an example, I was blessed to have one such organization at my own doorstep. When I was CEO of the United Methodist Church Foundation, I lived in San Antonio, Texas, the home base of the Socially Responsible Investment Coalition (SRIC). Working out of a suite of offices at the Oblate School of Theology on the Northside of San Antonio, SRIC rolls up its collective sleeves and takes the mystery out of the metrics of shareholder analysis. When a member provides its list of complete stock holdings, SRIC is able to analyze the policies, concerns, and corporate charters of companies held. Regional coalitions like SRIC keep databases of past engagements and current trends that allow members to join with others in dialogues and the filing of shareholder resolutions. It is important for your congregation and committee never to feel alone in this work of social change; finding and joining a regional coalition not only gives you the comfort of knowing that a larger organization has your back but also provides a network of others who are on the same or a similar journey.

Once any experience and expertise within your larger community has been gathered, some quick processing of priorities will be imperative to your engagement process. The conversation should begin with the highest or most central decision-making body within your congregation or organization, such as a board of directors, church council, common table, vestry, etc. The corporate engagement priorities should emerge from the theological perspectives and social justice initiatives within your current ministries or programs. For example, if your congregation has a childcare or school program onsite, you may want to prioritize the fight against human trafficking or child labor issues. Your congregation or organization should develop a list of no more than three to five priorities. Taking on more issues runs the risk of losing focus or spreading your resources too thin in an area of work that is new and unknown to many or all on your team.

Consider a bit of quick research in your denominational book of order, organization's bylaws, or charter to see if you are able to name an advisory member or two to your fiduciary committee. If so, you might consider a discussion with your pastoral or staff leaders about one or two members to join your fiduciary committee in a limited or advisory capacity, representing the programmatic, administrative, or advocacy work of your organization or congregation specifically for this work of shareholder advocacy. Your fiduciary committee members were chosen for expertise, experience, and inclusiveness. Often their backgrounds cover experience in law, finances, accounting, and business. As members of your congregation or organization, they surely also have passions for changing or repairing the world. The Jewish concept of *tikkun olam* found in the Mishnah comes to mind: "acts of kindness to perfect or repair the world." While existing members of your fiduciary committee may have that objective, it was likely not the quality that brought them to this particular area of service. Adding one or two advisory members even on a limited basis may prove valuable for many reasons beyond the choosing of priorities. Later in this chapter, we will explore the need to educate those in the pews and the community, as well as to encourage shareholder advocacy work by individuals and by other faith-based organizations. Advisory members at this early phase may prove of great benefit down the road.

One natural approach to compiling priorities for shareholder advocacy is to ask one or two members of your committee to poll the congregation's staff or lay leadership to amass a listing of ten to fifteen ministry priorities of your constituency. You might consider simultaneously assigning a different member or two to work with your regional coalition, or other resources, to identify ten to fifteen initiatives or areas of shareholder engagement already in process. Then use an agenda item at your next meeting to walk through both lists and to pair areas of engagement with ministry initiatives to derive three to five priorities for your work ahead.

Consider areas of ministry that connect with your congregation or organization in ways that already exist. For example, if women of your constituency have organized through denominational groups for local service or advocacy, or have been ordained as clergy from within your congregation or serve as a member of your pastoral team, consider a priority relating to gender rights issues or promoting the naming of women to boards of directors in companies owned. A surprising number of boards of publicly traded companies still have all-male membership. Some quick research online will yield lists of companies that have no women on their roster of board members. A few caveats: always double-check if the company's website does not feature photos of directors. Names are sometimes indeterminate of gender. Also, do some online research on the women you do find, especially if there is only one. "Overboarding" is a term that has emerged noting certain women and persons of color who serve on multiple boards. It is not that this is inherently bad, but electing the same woman over and over to various boards does not truly serve the intended goal of diversity. It also risks perpetuating a myth that there is only a small universe of women skilled to serve on publicly traded boards. It likely won't take you long in reviewing board rosters to find some names, of any gender identity, on more than one or even two boards. Also, beware of unwittingly setting an unfortunate precedent that "one is enough." Should your research lead you to a company or companies with no women among current directors, take the opportunity to explain the importance of shifting the culture as well as corporate governance policies to work toward gender parity in board membership. The goal should never be or be perceived as desiring just to elect one woman or person of color to a board. Inclusiveness on a board of directors is not limited, of course, to gender. It has often been observed that having one voice at a table will ensure that nothing will ever change! A male-dominated board with only one woman will be free to set discriminatory policy, always saying, "She was at the table when the decision was made." Surely that runs counter to your committee's and congregation's desired message and outcome.

As you have gathered in these last paragraphs, the same priority can be claimed for persons of color. One caveat here is to be careful to examine the history and tradition that your congregation/organization has claimed and, in many cases, endured to bring it to this priority. If you are reading this book, you are likely an American in an American religious organization or faith congregation. If so, you have inherited, like it or not, a very specific history of being enslaved or enslaving persons of African descent. Adopting a priority of furthering inclusion of persons of color on publicly traded boards is not furthered by inclusions of non-Americans of color. Global board membership and inclusion of a multinational perspective can be and surely is of vital importance to the strategies and business plan of most if not all publicly traded companies. However, that is not the driver for an effort to ensure the racial diversity of boards of American companies. One effective step might be for your committee process to discuss white privilege and the role it has played within your denomination, your congregation, and the companies that you own. A focus on white privilege and its impact may serve to narrow the deliverables or outcomes sought in making the inclusion of persons of color a priority. Again, if racial inclusiveness of publicly traded boards is a priority for you, be sure to research thoroughly the board membership of companies that you hold. Corporate governance pages or links on company websites always include short biographies of directors and sometimes photos. A telephone call to the investor services office will be a helpful step in your research.

In the priorities of both gender and racial diversity, I have conducted a dialogue session with a leading travel industry company, only to have its legal counsel espouse, "What do you mean? We have diversity on our board of directors! We have Democrats as well as Republicans!" I do not make this up; it happens. However, this vivid, if outrageous, anecdote emphasizes the strides to be made by making this area of advocacy a priority in your work. Other priorities ripe for picking include the reduction of reliance on fossil fuels, the fight against human trafficking, the reduction of availability of violent video games to youth and children, and food and water justice. A massive amount of resources and research will be at your fingertips through responsible investment coalitions. Sample resolutions, contact information, and metrics from past dialogues and engagements will be accessible to focus your work. Speaking of "your work," this leads easily to how you will be able to engage the top leadership, whether staff or directors, in the companies that you own.

Engage[1]

Now comes the "nuts and bolts" of the work at hand. The form of your ownership interests will determine your next steps. If you own interests in publicly traded companies through shares of mutual or pooled funds, this is an opportunity for some due diligence with the staff of funds owned. You should request quarterly or annual reports on shareholder advocacy activities such as proxy voting guidelines and actual votes. Also ask for similar reports on shareholder resolutions filed by the fund on behalf of its shareholders. If, however, you own shares of common or preferred stock directly, you can follow the overview below for filing a shareholder resolution.[2]

This is the part that often seems so mysterious or treacherous. Once you have been through your first two or three filings of shareholder resolutions, though, I am confident that you will chuckle that you ever thought it a challenge. The first step is to identify your direct holdings of stock of publicly traded companies. In order for your congregation or organization to file a resolution, you must continuously own at least $2,000 of the company's common or preferred stock in your congregation/organization's name for at least one year prior to filing. (Note that these standards may change over time. Please consult with your financial advisors or other appropriate

---

1. The following section is meant for informational purposes only, based on the extensive experience of the contributor, and should not be relied on as legal guidance. Before taking action on filing shareholder proposals, please consult your appropriate financial and legal advisors and the latest policies and guidance of the SEC as well as company policies on stocks you may own.

2. *Shareholder Proposals*, Securities and Exchange Commission, accessed August 4, 2019, *https://www.sec.gov/interps/legal/cfslb14g.htm* and *https://www.sec.gov/interps/legal/cfslb14i.htm*.

professionals or advocacy groups to confirm and clarify these particulars.) The holding cannot be through a mutual fund or a denominational or judicatory foundation. While you may pool with other record owners for the $2,000 minimum, based on current guidelines, your shares must be owned directly by your organization. Contact your investment advisor or custodian to ensure the status of ownership.[3] If you hold direct ownership of shares of only two to three dozen companies, your work may be more streamlined than originally thought. (See chapter 9 for ways to use a small portion of assets dedicated to the owning of individual shares and the possibility of inspiring donors.) Next, contact partners with whom you have established a relationship through membership or other alliances. You may want to provide their staff with a list of your holdings to assist in identifying existing engagements and resolutions that fit your priorities. Once you have found a handful of companies owned that have social concerns that fit within your priorities, you are ready to go!

Now is the time to do some quick and easy research on the companies' websites. In most cases, scroll to the bottom of the homepage, the menu of offices, or the "contact us" page and look for the investor services page. That page should provide you with the deadline date for filing a resolution. The deadline is usually 120 days or more prior to the scheduled annual meeting of stockholders, most of which are in the fall. Once you have calculated or located the date by which your resolution must be filed, look for the name, address, phone number, and fax number for the person to whom the resolution should be addressed. It is often but not always the corporate secretary. Shareholder services staff are sometimes quite helpful in providing some or all of this important information.

As soon as you have this information in hand, contact the custodian of your shares. If your investment advisor is a part of a major banking firm, your advisor and custodian may be the same; they likely are not. You will need a letter from your custodian confirming your direct ownership of shares on the date of your filing and that you have continuously owned at least $2,000 worth of stock for at least the preceding twelve months (or whatever the current standard is—please do follow up with your financial provider or supporting organization). For specific details on filing your resolution, you may wish to review the current protocols as listed on the Securities and Exchange Commission (SEC) website, www.sec.gov, or other resources.

---

3. *Shareholder Proposals*, Securities and Exchange Commission, accessed August 4, 2019, *https://www. sec.gov/interps/legal/cfslb14g.htm* and *https://www.sec.gov/interps/legal/cfslb14i.htm*.

The resolution wording is the hardest part and one for which your regional coalition or ICCR may be indispensable. You will almost never be the only faith-based organization to file a resolution on your priority issue. Others have filed and are filing the same resolutions. Even if you happen to be the sole filer, your regional coalition—or a local organization to assist members with resolutions as mentioned above—should assist in writing it.

Once you have identified the list of companies owned that fit your priority issues selected as set forth above, calendar the deadlines for filing. While they may be spread out in time over the year, they will most likely bunch in the late fall and winter. As soon as you calendar a deadline, do yourself and your custodian a favor and let them know of your need and your intended filing date. Custodians sometimes take some time to provide their confirmation letters. They are likely providing this service for many shareholders. They need advance notice, just as you do. Again, check the SEC's published or online references at www.sec.gov for specific information on timelines and processes for drafting and submitting proposals.

Naturally, the company will feel it is in their best interests to resolve a shareholder's concerns prior to that time to avoid having to include it in the proxy materials. Through a dialogue process, a company's board of directors may agree to make a change that satisfies your priority issue, at least as a significant step. If agreeable with the proposed change in behavior, policy, or reporting, the requested action on your part will be to withdraw the resolution, which you will need to do in writing, typically by e-mail. If agreement is not reached, your resolution will be printed in the proxy statement for the annual meeting of stockholders. The lead filer must ensure that a person attends the meeting and presents the resolution from the floor of the meeting for vote by stockholders. Know that resolutions that originate from shareholders are advisory only and not binding on the company's board of directors.

As annual meetings of all of your companies owned approach, initiate conversation with your investment advisor and custodian to ascertain how proxies are received, processed, voted, and reported. Proxies are the mechanisms for you, as a direct owner of shares, to cast your vote on all matters that impact corporate governance. Proxies include the annual election of members of the board of directors of a company, appointment of external audit firms, and shareholder resolutions. If you don't get a quick answer, investigate. You want to be sure that you are clear about how your organization communicates to companies owned on all issues contained in proxy statements, including proposals initiated by a board of directors or by a shareholder. Proxy voting can be a valued part of stock ownership, and your membership or constituency should be advised of any resolutions filed and when proxy voting materials can be expected in case they own shares of the same companies.

Educate

As your investing congregation begins to engage with public companies, whether through direct shareholder engagement, dialogues, or voting proxies, perhaps the most important step that can be undertaken will be to educate your members. This education process can take several forms and should include as many communication channels as possible. Those channels should include the pulpit, the classroom, the website, and the regular periodic communications within the congregation.

First, if the clergy leadership of your congregation are not already a part of the fiduciary process that led to the engagement, frequent and regular consultation with them is a *sine qua non* at several levels. A congregation's clergy leaders have a unique outlet to teach and share examples of love and justice within the life of the congregation. While the province of preaching and worship planning accountability lies uniquely with the pastoral staff, they cannot preach about what they don't know! Nothing can replace the inclusion of clergy leadership in every step of the conversation that leads to effective corporate engagement. However, their time is limited and their full participation in meetings and dialogue sessions is rarely a possibility. Keeping all clergy members apprised of all steps in the engagement process will pay dividends. Of course, clergy preach, but they also write regular columns, web articles, and blogs. They meet with other clergy and they have access to other channels of communications within the ecclesial connection within a judicatory or denomination.

Speaking of communication channels, the fiduciary committee that engages with public companies needs to keep in regular contact with the congregation's webmaster, blogger, and media staff. It may be as simple as a weekly newsletter that is administered by e-mail, listserv, or web application. However, in today's world of social and electronic media, more and more congregations have opportunities to share sound bites about news within the congregation via various online media such as Facebook, Twitter, texting applications, and television programming. It may well be too late to make those connections with communicators once engagement has begun or has completed, whether judged to have been successful or not. Those channels need to be prepared for news of engagements and need to be looking for information as it unfolds. Examples of these channels include the worship bulletin, weekly newsletters, bulletin boards, video monitors in worship services or entry halls, welcome desks, and staff missives.

In addition to official congregational communication outlets, lay leaders who have been involved in the engagement work should develop talking points to be used on their own social media and e-mail, and for speaking engagements within the congregation, ecumenical community, and regional coalitions. (Potentially, many donors who support similar initiatives may be inspired to give to the congregation/entity because of your efforts. See chapter 9.) In some instances, secular press will be interested in shareholder engagement success on behalf of a congregation or faith-based organization. While those contacts are often best left to professional media or communications staff, fiduciary committee members should use talking points to make the most efficient use of precious media time. It is important for communications and education to be on the agenda of fiduciary committee meetings from an early point in engagement planning.

Encourage

Within the education process throughout and beyond the congregation or primary constituency lies an opportunity for you to encourage others to live out their faith and values similarly. Surely we have the responsibility to inspire others to engage public corporations by sharing information about the steps, process, and successes of our engagements. Other congregations and faith-based groups within denominational connections, as well as the ecumenical community that directly hold shares of public companies, have likely been under the same misconceptions described earlier. By educating those around your process about your engagement, you will incite them to take action as well. However, know that you will need to be prepared to provide helpful materials and information to assist them in their engagements. Part of that information will surely be a connection to any local or regional coalition that works in the SRI area, especially with shareholder engagements.

This opportunity and responsibility to encourage others to take action likewise is not limited to other congregations and institutional investors. Investors holding shares of publicly traded companies surely sit in your pews and at your board tables. As with any area of stewardship, or how we are called to care for our neighbors and world through our actions, your fiduciary committee should seize this opportunity to inspire and challenge individuals and families to live their faith through the ways that they invest their money. If your committee felt that shareholder engagement was beyond your grasp, imagine how individual shareholders feel. Many individual shareholders, with or without the assistance of a local or regional coalition, do regularly take the steps to file shareholder resolutions that are presented in proxy statements and voted by shareholders. As discussed above, this is an effective way to get the attention of management as well as owners. Your fiduciary committee should be prepared to go beyond issuing press releases, circulars, and statements about engagements and successes and should provide simple guidelines. By sharing this "how-to" information, you will demystify and simplify the process for others. The reach of local and regional coalitions is as robust as their budgets allow. But rarely will they have the ability to reach individuals living their faith within your congregation or organization.

Think of groups that already meet within the life of your organization. Classes; women's, men's, and youth groups; and study or focus groups are often looking for new material for study that approaches faith, good deeds, or mitzvahs from a new angle. Shareholder advocacy through corporate engagement is likely a new and fresh topic that would be welcomed if properly supported. Members of your fiduciary committee would likely need to be available to assist in leading discussions. Materials, even as simple as your meeting agenda from your engagement process, will be valuable assists for inspiring conversation and action.

As you consider initial steps that your fiduciary committee in your local church, parish, or faith-based organization might take to put your faith into action with the publicly traded companies that you own, remember this call to empower, engage, educate, and encourage. None should feel alone in this effort or that they are inventing the first wheel. Others of faith have gone before and will provide significant help. The steps for accountability to the central decision-making body of the congregation or organization not only ensure appropriate approval processes but also are a means of sharing information for record keeping and corporate memory. By taking the first step, you and your congregation or organization will join a heritage of shareholder advocacy of leveraging financial holdings for social change and a more just world.

Chapter 5

Inclusion, Equity, and Diversity*

Carsten W. Sierck

Every choice a church makes reveals its values and priorities. That sounds like a heavy burden, but it has been the foundation of faith-based, or faith*ful*, investing for ages. Over the years, many churches and other faith-based groups have committed to avoid investing in businesses that conflict with their moral values—no weapons, no tobacco, and no gambling, among others. Some call these "sin stocks" and will not have anything to do with them.

Faith-based values are broader, though, and include ideas of participation and welcome. Who participates in the life of the church? How do we welcome newcomers? Can we be sure we make room for all? These ideas of inclusion are important. They are a foundation of many Christian denominations. From Romans 15:7: "Welcome one another, therefore, just as Christ has welcomed you, for the glory of God."

Many congregations try hard to include everyone. They have nursery programs and senior luncheons, handicapped access and sign language interpretation. Some proudly proclaim a radical welcome, and others make space for community groups. As they govern themselves, develop programming, and manage resources, many churches also aim to include a variety of voices among their leadership. And some of the savviest know they can put their investments to work to promote inclusion as well as provide a financial return to support church ministry and programming.

If you would like your church or faith-based group to be inclusive, to promote diversity, and to foster a more equitable society, and you would like to use its investment strategy as one way to work toward those goals, here are some things to think about.

---

* This material, including organizations and websites noted, is provided for informational purposes only and should not be viewed as an endorsement or as investment, tax, or other professional advice.

What's the Context?

All investors invest their assets for financial return. For churches, this provides support for mission and ministry beyond what they receive as pledges or other annual gifts. But some investors also invest for social change, knowing that their money gives them power and that investors have influence, especially when they work together. Some churches also invest to make a statement, aware that every choice a church makes reflects its values. They want their investments to align with their faith, and they are investing to do good.

Investing to promote inclusion and diversity is part of *ESG investing*—that is, investing with an eye toward various environmental, social, and governance concerns. This is a type of socially responsible investing that came along after efforts to screen out "sin stocks" and other undesirable companies. The goal is to encourage companies of all kinds to *improve* how they address pressing issues, how they adapt to social change, and how they manage themselves. To accomplish this, investors must *engage* with companies, not only making an initial decision to invest in a company but also examining over time how a company can do better in the face of new developments at the company, in its business, or in a wider corporate or social context. Examples of this kind of engagement are given below, but it is important to understand why this is an important kind of socially responsible investing.

At first, faith-based and other investors wanted to avoid investing in—and supporting—companies that did not suit their values: weapons manufacturers, for example, or those doing business in South Africa. This approach remains compelling for many. In the aggregate, withholding funds from companies with objectionable businesses or policies may bring negative publicity to those companies, might eventually reduce available capital, and could pressure them to change their business or operations.

But some investors began to think more broadly. They wanted to encourage companies to do better. They understood that the actions of corporations can have a sizable impact. They wanted them to reduce damage to the environment, or improve working conditions, or modernize their management practices. Some wanted to encourage forward-thinking companies to lead the way in adopting sound business practices. Others recognized that we need certain products—energy, for example—but we can try to improve the way we get what we need. Still others wanted to invest in broad market indexes without screening out companies but also use their power as investors to encourage positive change.

Many recent and respected investment studies—in particular McKinsey's widely cited 2015 report, *Diversity Matters*[1]—have concluded that companies that adopted sustainable environmental policies, took stock of the impact of their business on all stakeholders and society more broadly, and adopted good governance practices were likely to outperform those that did not. These companies have examined and evaluated threats to their business, disclosed the risks publicly, and are making strides to adopt policies that are more sustainable. This type of investing—ESG investing—now drives a sizable amount of socially responsible investing as investors seek both strong returns *and* social benefits.

More specifically, environmental concerns might include climate change, carbon emissions, air pollution, waste management, water scarcity, and deforestation, among many others. Social considerations often address human rights, labor standards, community relations, and issues of gender equity and diversity. Governance concerns often center on ensuring that corporate leaders hear from a variety of voices so that they do not insulate themselves from challenge or change. Issues include board composition and independence, executive compensation, whistleblower protections, audit committee composition, anticorruption policies, and more. Clearly, these concerns are central to sound and sustainable business, but for many they also reflect a desirable set of values.

The expansion of socially responsible investing to include ESG considerations dramatically increases the ways that faith-based investors can work for change. By joining a movement of other socially minded investors—and investors seeking to improve investment returns—they can set new expectations for corporate policy and practice, using the annual meeting proxy process as well as direct dialogue and public relations campaigns (see chapter 4). Thus, for the many churches, religious groups, and spiritually focused investors of all faiths who hold high the ideals of inclusion and diversity and equity, there is no time like now to invest for change.

Investment managers, coalition groups, large foundations, and other investors are raising the issues, explaining the benefits, and encouraging change. Churches of all sizes can participate too. Many of the examples in this chapter highlight engagement and activism by investment managers or coalition groups, but some investment managers and denominational foundations are also developing various types of screened funds. This chapter includes a sample of various methods and results.

---

1. Vivian Hunt, Dennis Layton, and Sara Prince, *Diversity Matters* (McKinsey & Company, February 2, 2015), *https://assets.mckinsey.com/~/media/857F440109AA4D13A54D9C496D86ED58.ashx.*

One detail: this change is incremental but over time may lead to a remarkable transformation, not only within companies but also across broader groups as standards and expectations are reset. ESG investors are working *with* companies to encourage them to monitor, review, report, and adapt corporate practices, one issue at a time. Small changes add up, and small changes over time across a collection of companies or an entire industry can have a broad impact, changing standard practices, setting new investor and societal expectations, and spurring further incremental change.

What Are the Issues?

Inclusion, diversity, equity: many of us believe in them all, but together they combine to become a very large topic. It may seem hard to know where to begin, where it might even be possible to make a difference. As a guide, here are some of the primary issues today in investing for inclusion.

Corporate Leadership Diversity

Companies with diverse leaders are more successful, as noted in McKinsey's *Diversity Matters*. They attract top talent, strengthen customer orientation, increase employee satisfaction, improve decision-making, and enhance the company's image. This correlates to improved financial performance. A subsequent McKinsey report, *Delivering through Diversity*,[2] asserts that the relationship between diversity and performance persists, leadership roles matter, and all forms of diversity make a difference.

Diversity on corporate boards of directors is a current focus of many ESG investors. As noted by the CEO of BlackRock, one of the world's largest investment managers:

> Boards with a diverse mix of genders, ethnicities, career experiences, and ways of thinking have, as a result, a more diverse and aware mindset. They are less likely to succumb to groupthink or miss new threats to a company's business model. And they are better able to identify opportunities that promote long-term growth.[3]

---

2. Vivian Hunt, Sara Prince, Sundiatu Dixon-Fyle, and Lareina Yee, *Delivering through Diversity* (McKinsey & Company, January 2018), *https://www.mckinsey.com/~/media/McKinsey/Business%20 Functions/Organization/Our%20Insights/Delivering%20through%20diversity/Delivering-through-diversity_ full-report.ashx.*

3. "A Sense of Purpose: Larry Fink's 2018 Letter to CEOs," BlackRock, accessed June 23, 2019, *https://www.blackrock.com/corporate/investor-relations/2018-larry-fink-ceo-letter.*

Board diversity is easy for investors to measure and publicize, making it a good place to start to advocate for inclusion. And there is a strong financial—and public relations—case to be made for change. Investors already have the right to weigh in on board composition—they must approve the nomination of directors to the board. It is possible that this could become less perfunctory than before, or that corporate leaders hoping to head off an unwanted shareholder proposal might ensure board diversity in advance of any challenge.

There is also the issue of diversity among corporate *executives*. This can lead to reduced "groupthink," increased creativity, and better risk management, according to a recent Catalyst study, *Quick Take: Why Diversity and Inclusion Matter.*[4] This is just as important for investors working toward both social and financial goals, yet it is harder to influence. It is less public because it is typically left to the sole discretion of corporate boards and senior management; shareholders do not get to vote on CEOs and other leaders. While there is no formal role for investors to play, they can still influence the policies of boards of directors who oversee and advise management generally.

But with both types of diversity—on boards and among executives—come the broader social benefits that many investors, including many faith-based investors, desire. Within their companies, diverse corporate leaders can ensure the hiring and retention of a diverse set of employees. They can do this by creating, implementing, and monitoring corporate policy and establishing formal and informal mentoring arrangements. Outside their companies, diverse corporate leaders may become community leaders and role models. Both results help create opportunity and improve participation in the economic life of our country.

In these areas, engagement is often a better strategy than screening. Many churches and others investing for social change will want to remain invested in a broadly diversified portfolio across all major asset classes and industry sectors. Currently, there are some key economic sectors—technology, for example—where gender diversity in leadership lags.[5] Many investors will not want to miss the opportunity to invest in these areas and instead will opt to use engagement and advocacy to promote change. It is a chance to improve rather than rebuke.

---

4. "Why Diversity and Inclusion Matter: Quick Take," Catalyst, August 1, 2018, *https://www.catalyst.org/research/why-diversity-and-inclusion-matter.*

5. Judith Warner, Nora Ellmann, and Diana Boesch, "The Women's Leadership Gap," Center for American Progress, November 20, 2018, *https://www.americanprogress.org/issues/women/reports/2018/11/20/461273/womens-leadership-gap-2/.*

Workplace Diversity

More broadly, but for similar reasons, faith-based investors may wish to promote inclusion, equity, and diversity at *all* levels of a company. Indeed, companies with poor gender diversity across all levels of employees face reputational, business, and operational risks they should be encouraged to avoid. They may be subject to discrimination lawsuits, have limited insight when making business decisions, and have trouble attracting and retaining employees. Investors may choose to influence corporate hiring practices by encouraging disclosure, sharing best practices, or using shareholder resolutions to force change.

Companies committed to workplace diversity must put in place workplace policies that protect and support a diverse employee base. These might include hiring practices, equal pay standards, antiharassment procedures, and objective internal grievance procedures.

What Are Other Investors Doing?

Here are some examples of what other investors are doing to promote inclusion, equity, and diversity in the workplace. Some of these investors are investment managers acting on behalf of a wide range of clients who have delegated their voting power. Others are concerned groups promoting a social, development, or faith-based agenda. Most broadly, tactics include analyzing and rating corporate performance, engaging with companies to share best practices and encourage change, asking for more disclosure, voting proxies in favor of diversity, submitting shareholder proposals, and agreeing to withdraw them if companies adopt new policies. Unlike in the past, some investment managers today are becoming apostles of corporate change. It is perfectly acceptable to ask what *your* investment manager is doing.

Corporate Leadership Diversity

Shareholder Resolutions

Recently, a coalition of faith-based investors submitted various shareholder resolutions to promote diversity on corporate boards of directors. Many of these proposals asked companies to include qualified minority and female candidates on an initial list of possible directors, pointing to the significant relationship between racial diversity and innovation, reputation, and firm performance. In other cases, the coalition requested that companies report on steps to enhance board diversity, such as formally committing to diversify the board in terms of gender, race, ethnicity, and sexual orientation, committing publicly to include diverse candidates, and disclosing its process for identifying diverse candidates. Its focus is on building board accountability on this issue.

The coalition has also submitted shareholder resolutions to promote diversity of all kinds among executive leaders. These require boards of directors to evaluate current levels of diversity and develop and share a plan to increase racial, ethnic, *and* gender diversity among executives. The idea here, of course, is that what you measure, you work on, and what you must publicize, you may decide to change.

Corporate Engagement

One of the world's largest institutional asset managers has a robust asset stewardship program of corporate engagement and shareholder activism, including very public efforts intended to change the corporate mindset on diversity. It has in 2 years called on more than 1,200 companies with no women on their boards to act. More than 300 companies have added women. And a key priority in 2019 for the asset stewardship program is to review how companies disclose information about their diversity practices and metrics.

Proxy Voting Guidelines

The proxy voting guidelines of another investment manager state that it expects to see two women directors on every corporate board. Yet another has escalated its engagement efforts and recently announced that, beginning in 2020, it would vote against the nominating committee's entire slate of nominees to the board if a company has no women on the board and has not responded to encouragement to change. Here, the investment manager is focusing on the process for nominating directors as a supplement to its efforts to highlight the bias that undervalues the workplace contributions of women.

Screened Funds

One investment manager has developed a gender diversity index that tracks the performance of large US companies that lead their industry sectors in including women on boards of directors and in executive leadership positions. This, or similar indexes developed elsewhere, can become the foundation of funds that invest primarily in companies leading gender diversity efforts—funds that screen positively for diversity and inclusion.

Workplace Diversity

Corporate Engagement

The Fair Chance Hiring Campaign sets out best practices around ensuring that those with criminal backgrounds have a chance to work. A report from the National Employment Law Project shows that not only has the US economy lost billions because people with criminal records could not work, but employment is the single-most important factor in reducing recidivism. Various tech companies have created executive positions focused on diversity and inclusion in response to shareholder pressure to address a heavily male workforce. And some investors are challenging tech companies to tie CEO pay to racial and gender equity.

Shareholder Resolutions

To improve diversity at all levels in the financial services industry—in which women and people of color remain under-represented in professional roles—one group of activist shareholders brought resolutions requiring a company to share statistics about its workforce composition and a description of policies and programs intended to increase diversity hiring. It introduced similar resolutions at another company with a history of large payouts to settle discrimination lawsuits. Several years ago, it asked companies operating in states that allow discrimination based on sexual orientation to report on the risks of doing business in those states. Other investor initiatives have focused on paid family leave.

These are important social issues, and they fall clearly within the context of ESG investing. Even more clearly, these issues go directly toward inclusion, equity, and diversity, key concerns for many faith-based investors who want to use their investments to promote the values of their faith. Recently, the focus on ESG investing has intensified, but while many companies are indeed committing to improve diversity and equity, it will take time to learn how effective the implementation of new policies and procedures will be.

Does Any of This Make a Difference?

Here is the nineteenth-century Unitarian clergyman Edward Everett Hale:

> I am only one; but still I am one. I can't do everything; but still I can do some-
> thing; and because I cannot do everything, I will not refuse to do the something
> that I can do.[6]

For many adults, their work and their workplaces are a center point of their lives. Countless hours are spent at work, with work colleagues, watching managers and leaders show through words and deeds what really matters at the organization. Companies and organizations of all kinds—large and small, for-profit and not-for-profit, old and established and scrappy new startups—create their own cultures and influence how employees think about a variety of issues.

Investors who push companies to be more inclusive, equitable, and diverse help drive this change. Results may take time—remember this is incremental change—but a series of small steps, starting with a company acknowledging an issue's importance, adopting a policy to address it, and then implementing new procedures, is an important way to start. More broadly, these efforts can influence public expectations and related policy.

Here is a small sample of recent developments:

- California passed a law in 2018 requiring publicly traded companies headquartered in California to have women on their boards of directors.

- A major retailer has achieved gender and race pay equity in the United States—male and female employees are paid the same and employees of different races are paid the same—and is now working to achieve that inter-nationally. It is also sharing with other companies the principles and tools it uses. And recently, other large employers have joined that company in a commitment to pay equity. Note that in the past, this company has been the target of significant shareholder activism around workplace inequality.

- Another corporation has announced that senior executives will play a direct role in setting the company's racial and gender inclusion strategy. It too has been the focus of shareholder activism and public pressure around its lack of diversity.

---

6. Quoted in Jeanie A. B. Greenough, *A Year of Beautiful Thoughts* (New York: Thomas Y. Crowell & Co., 1902), 172 (digitized by Google).

- A multinational chain has agreed to publish its policies and procedures to correct pay disparities among workers of different genders, races, and ethnicities after considerable shareholder pressure.

- A manufacturer agreed to publicize its policy that it will consider background—including age, gender, nationality, race, ethnicity, and specialized experience—as it conducts board searches. This was in response to a shareholder proposal, later withdrawn, to encourage greater board diversity.

Shareholder engagement can prompt change. Sharing best practices and current expectations, encouraging companies to change accepted practices, and submitting shareholder proposals to force the issues can make a difference. And the positive and negative publicity that may result can further encourage change. Investors who encourage companies to have diverse leaders and inclusive workplaces help shape our society. They want to see direct and measurable results, of course, but they are also hoping—whether articulated in this way or not—to see our country's financial capital used to help shape a more equitable society. At the same time, investors encouraging change also raise broader awareness of these issues and may cause a public relations issue for some companies. At some point, shareholder engagement may encourage the general public to demand change.

How Can I Invest in This Way?

How are interested faith-based investors to know what to do? How do they keep up with the research? Know what companies to try to influence? Make themselves heard? And how do the busy volunteer members of church committees ever find the time? How about this . . . choose an investment manager who is attuned to these concerns, who has a program of corporate engagement, who can use its size to have influence, or who joins with other concerned investors to understand these issues and work for change. Or choose an investment manager who makes available investments that favor companies working toward inclusion, equity, and diversity. You might also take a look at what your denominational foundation offers.

More broadly, church leaders—lay and clergy, paid and volunteer—and interested members of the congregation will want to learn about these issues and build consensus that investing for environmental, social, and governance concerns is important. For some, corporate engagement and activism may be a new way to think about socially responsible investing. For others who have been focused on traditional "sin stocks," ESG considerations may also be new to them. Maybe not everyone thinks inclusion is important enough to pursue. Maybe someone is skeptical about results. But as ESG investing has evolved from novelty to orthodoxy among many wise investors, it is important for churches to consider it. There may be agreement or disagreement on the specifics, but the discussion itself, in the church community and beyond, is important.

Communication with the congregation is essential. Talk about the faith imperative for inclusion. Discuss how many of the faithful follow reflection with action. Foster support for using church investments in tandem with other efforts to encourage diversity. And for the skeptics among us, discuss the power of incremental change. It may be hard to know where to start to create the equitable society our faiths demand, but start somewhere we must. Small steps added together over time can change what is acceptable, and over time they can add up to significant, enduring change. And this can be change that reflects the enduring values of our faiths.

From Theodore Roosevelt: "Do what you can, with what you have, where you are."[7]

---

7. Theodore Roosevelt, *An Autobiography* (New York: MacMillan, 1913), 34.

Chapter 6

Dignity of Every Human Being– Human Rights, Human Trafficking, and Investing*

*Séamus P. Finn***

Introduction

The dignity of each human being as created in the image and likeness of God—as it is found in the genesis stories of the scriptures—is the foundation and inspiration for many of the issues that are priorities for faith traditions as they seek to align the mission, administration, and operation of their various institutions, including the management of their assets, with their beliefs and values. While recognizing that Adam and Eve were driven from paradise because they turned against God and were obliged to till the earth and to survive by the sweat of their brow, the Hebrew Scriptures nevertheless go on to articulate a basic set of codes and expectations to govern behavior for relationships between human beings, and between human beings and Creation, that would allow them to live their lives consistent with God's providence. In addition, codes and laws were eventually articulated and adopted to govern any financial contracts or relationships or commercial transactions that were undertaken between human beings in the marketplace.

For centuries the teaching and traditions that were articulated and employed were tested and adapted through the experiences of the followers of the faith tradition in different regions, localities, and situations across the

---

* This material, including organizations and websites noted, is provided for informational purposes only and should not be viewed as an endorsement or as investment, tax, or other professional advice.

** Editor's note: This chapter focuses on the history and progress made through legislation and collaboration among investors and various organizations, including the United Nations and other international entities. The chapter also highlights the context and importance of increasing shareholder knowledge on these topics, as well as the many resources now available to investors.

world, and they were debated and refined in religious and public assemblies. Through this iterative process, customs and regulations evolved into principles that were formally adopted and became part of the different codes of laws and precepts that were enforced in the marketplace and throughout society. These rules were also applied to enumerate the rights and responsibilities of parties in borrowing and lending transactions and the duties and responsibilities of partners in joint ownership structures.

Frequently, whether in terms of time and the primordial act of Creation by God or the appeal to respecting the divine intention for all of Creation, we are reminded that we live in an interdependent web of life that includes all living beings and generations yet unborn. This perspective also applies to our treatment and responsible care for Creation and the numerous ways in which the living natural world is a part of our lives. (The environment through the lens of climate change will be specifically addressed in the following chapter and referenced in other sections.) As we grow more and more aware of the essential nature of our interdependence on the environment and the earth, it is critical that the implications of this perspective be integrated into the construction of any commercial or financial transactions.

Human beings and all of Creation were taken as a given in applying the different codes and principles that have been referenced above, but the divine origin of all was presupposed throughout. In this chapter we will focus primarily on human dignity and on how protecting, respecting, and promoting human dignity must be a core priority in evaluating the moral responsibility of those participating in financial and commercial transactions. This responsibility extends to those who are shareholders in these enterprises and funds. We will also examine how human rights issues entered into the engagements that shareholders initiated with corporations and the process whereby human rights policies were developed and strengthened. This will include the role that shareholders, civil society, and the formal public sector held in this process.

Human Rights as an Expression of Human Dignity

The stranger, the alien, the widow, and the migrant were singled out for the special treatment of care throughout the scriptures, though they were given much less protection and care in most societies because of their perceived lower status. In addition, slavery and indentured servitude, which included trafficking in human beings for a variety of purposes, were often practiced and seen as the bounty that was part of the spoils collected by conquering armies.

In hindsight it must be recognized that these practices which were conceived through a process that justified discrimination based on race, gender, religion, and ethnicity were immediately in violation of the fundamental belief that all human beings were created in the image and likeness of God. There is plenty of evidence to demonstrate the many ways where the basic dignity and human rights of those in a subservient status were violated through a system of stereotyping because of race, gender, religion, or place of origin. Addressing this dichotomy between religious beliefs and common practice in some societies has remained an ongoing challenge that needs to be addressed.

The practice of slavery, forms of indentured servitude, and human trafficking are some of the most egregious violations of human dignity. They would over the centuries find their way into many different sectors of society, including domestic service and the agriculture, manufacturing, and service sectors. They were practiced and facilitated in a variety of different forms that became carefully organized into global networks of human trafficking and can still be found operating around the world today.

Forced labor frequently takes advantage of groups of people who are suffering from dire economic situations or lack of education; they see little opportunity for advancement in their own regions or countries and are therefore forced to migrate. Especially for those that are employed on the land, advances in technology and instant communication facilitate the quick movement of those under forced labor, making their abuse less visible and not immediately obvious to authorities.

Responding to the Industrial Revolution: Human Rights

The rapid expansion of the Industrial Revolution, whereby the manufacturing process was consolidated into big factories organized around a system that needed reliable access to raw materials, energy, and a plentiful supply of steady labor, would present a unique set of challenges and opportunities. The relationship between employees and employers as well as the rights and responsibilities of both the workers and the owners of these expanding manufacturing processes, became a high priority. In many instances the incoming workers were young and came directly from the agricultural sector or from the waves of foreign immigrants that were migrating to the United States.

The working conditions for all these factory workers would attract the attention of the faith traditions wherever these large-scale industrial factories became a fixture across Europe and North America and later when they expanded throughout the world. These concerns evolved from many of the foundational teachings about the proper treatment of domestic servants or agricultural workers in an earlier period and were expanded to address the specific conditions that existed in these factories. The issues that were identified included the age of the workers, the adequacy of the wages being paid, and the number of hours worked balanced with the appropriate free time to fulfill any other family obligations that the workers had. Safety and security both in the places of work and the operation of any equipment, especially motorized equipment, were also considered.

The right of workers to form associations to protect their interests in the bargaining process about working conditions and the items mentioned above would be identified by religious traditions as being in need of special protection, given the unequal position that individuals bargaining on their own faced in those situations. The promotion and protection of these rights are practical examples of how religious leaders applied the considered human dignity and human rights through the lens of the Hebrew and Christian scriptures.

In 1891, as a result of the repositioning and restructuring of labor that was taking place during the period of the Industrial Revolution and the numerous abuses that resulted in the campaigns to protect workers and to ensure respect for their rights, Pope Leo XIII in the encyclical *Rerum Novarum*[1] listed a number of specific issues and protections that needed attention. In this document, he set out a foundation for protecting and respecting the rights and responsibilities of employers and employees.

The establishment of the International Labor Organization (ILO) in 1919 was a clear indication that many of the concerns raised by faith traditions were also shared by governments and civil society. This collaborative body, which included representatives of governments, employers, and employees with broad international support, would be instrumental in laying the foundation for many of the themes and topics that were captured in the teaching of the faith traditions that saw human rights as an expression of human dignity.

The fundamental priorities that were grounded in the beliefs of different faith traditions were further solidified in international law by the

---

1. Leo XIII, Encyclical Letter *Rerum Novarum*, May 15, 1891, *http://w2.vatican.va/content/leo-xiii/en/encyclicals/documents/hf_l-xiii_enc_15051891_rerum-novarum.html.*

United Nations. In the Universal Declaration of Human Rights (UDHR)[2] that emerged from the United Nations in 1948, we see what some have described as a watershed "in the process of liberation" from material, political economic, and social bondage and an affirmation of how human dignity is protected through respecting human rights.[3] This affirmation by all those represented in the UN process was given additional explicit practical expression in the insistence that among those rights were political and civil, economic, social, and cultural rights.

In 2011, the UN Human Rights Council unanimously endorsed the Guiding Principles on Business and Human Rights (UNGPs),[4] which was the first framework for corporate human rights responsibility recognized by the United Nations. The UNGPs consist of thirty-one principles implementing the United Nations "Protect, Respect, and Remedy" framework on human rights and transnational corporations and other enterprises. They provide therefore the first global standard for addressing the risk of adverse impacts on human rights that are related to business and business operations. They also provide an internationally accepted framework for enhancing standards and practices regarding business and human rights.

The UNGPs include three pillars that are designed to outline the framework that should be implemented by states and businesses:

- The state duty to protect human rights;
- The corporate responsibility to respect human rights;
- Access to remedy for victims of business-related abuses[5]

Protecting the Dignity and Rights of the Indigenous

The recognition of the human dignity and rights of indigenous peoples was a much slower and more protracted debate within the international community and UN system. Each country followed a different path in relationships

---

2. "Universal Declaration of Human Rights," United Nations, accessed May 28, 2019, *https://www. un.org/en/universal-declaration-human-rights/*.

3. Mathew A. Shadle, *Interrupting Capitalism: Catholic Social Thought and the Economy* (New York: Oxford University Press, 2018), 64–65.

4. "UN Guiding Principles," Business and Human Rights Resource Centre, accessed May 28, 2019, *https://www.business-humanrights.org/en/un-guiding-principles*.

5. "UN Guiding Principles on Business and Human Rights (UNGPs)," Europa.eu, accessed May 28, 2019, *https://europa.eu/capacity4dev/platform-rmsc-garment-sector/document/un-guiding-principles-business-and-human-rights-ungps*.

with the indigenous populations that lived within their commonly recognized sovereign boundaries. These approaches ranged from forceful and violent strategies to suppress them completely or confine them to settlements or reserves, to more restrained approaches that tried to follow negotiated paths to peaceful coexistence. These negotiations are ongoing in numerous jurisdictions throughout the world.

At the United Nations level, after more than eight decades of pleas for the recognition of the unique status of the indigenous within the international system, some milestones were achieved with the adoption in 1989 of convention 169, "Indigenous and Tribal Peoples Convention," in the ILO system and the adoption of the "UN Declaration on the Rights of Indigenous Peoples" (UNDRIP) by the General Assembly on September 13, 2007.[6] The declaration is a resolution and not a law-bearing document. Indigenous people are not considered a country and do not have the right to the protection of international law through the international court of justice. However, article 40 clearly states that indigenous peoples have the right to fair procedures for the resolution of conflicts and disputes with countries or other parties, because indigenous people are not afforded access to the international court of justice.

The protection of the human dignity and human rights of indigenous people, however, is deserving of more specific attention by the faith-based and responsible investor. In the first instance, for the faith-based investor, there are many parallels between the ways that the indigenous have been treated since the adoption of the sovereign state system and the treatment afforded to strangers, foreigners, servants, and minorities in the scriptures. Secondly, the numerous times when the indigenous have been dispossessed of their land and subject to violent and horrendous acts of suppression is demonstrably contradictory of the teachings of the scriptures. Thirdly, our ancestors in the faith were often complicit in the many acts of injustice perpetrated by civil authorities against them.

More proximate in the current day and for all responsible investors, the lives and livelihoods of indigenous communities intersect frequently with the business plans of corporations, especially in some specific sectors. This is immediately obvious when the business of a corporation involves the ancestral lands that are home to the indigenous and how their rights are respected throughout the contracting and exploratory process. The mining, oil, and

---

6. "UN Declaration on the Rights of Indigenous Peoples," Australian Human Rights Commission, accessed May 28, 2019, *https://www.humanrights.gov.au/publications/un-declaration-rights-indigenous-peoples-1*.

gas sectors are examples because of their large-scale disruptive business operations, as are any of the forestry and agribusiness projects that seek to operate in indigenous territories. The routes that roads and pipelines take to transport products, especially if they traverse burial grounds and sacred sites, are also relevant.

Respect for the spiritual and cultural identity and traditions of indigenous people is sometimes an issue in many of the marketing and brand dimensions of various enterprises. The names and logos of sports teams come immediately to mind, as do the images and portrayals of the indigenous, their ancestors, and their traditions in movies and television, many of these still broadcast on mass media even though they were produced decades ago.

Globalization of the Manufacturing Process and Human Rights

The intervening seventy-plus years since the Universal Declaration of Human Rights has resulted in a deeper understanding of the basic human rights that were identified in the declaration and an extensive exploration of their implications for the relationships between governments, citizens, and the indigenous, and the relationships between owners, managers, and workers in the commercial and financial sectors. Over these intervening decades each sovereign nation has also been urged to customize for their own jurisdictions the obligations that they assumed when they signed on to any or all of the nine treaties of the declaration, to apply them in their respective countries and jurisdictions, and to cooperate with the UN Universal Periodic Review process by other sovereign signatories.

Among the three ingredients of capital, raw material, and labor that are necessary for a business to succeed, the cost of labor has varied significantly from country to country over time. The multinational expansion of businesses, especially the manufacturing part of their operations as they search for new sources of cheaper labor and reliable access to raw materials, intersected at several junctures with local labor and human rights laws and the obligations that countries had assumed through the UDHR process. This would lead to periodic shifts of factories and production either from one region or one country to another and resulted in subsequent debates about the harmonization of applicable human rights and labor policies. In addition, these movements in the manufacturing and production process were often encouraged and supported by new trade agreements, advances in technology, significant reductions in the costs for transportation, and the search for more stable political circumstances.

The list of the basic issues and challenges that surfaced in factories and between workers and owners would remain consistent. Wages, safety, working age, working hours, leisure time, freedom of association, and discrimination, though open to differing interpretations and regulated according to local laws and customs, were universal concerns. Addressing these issues would become more complicated when the process of production of the final product was managed through a series of multiple sourcing arrangements that could touch every step in the process. Employment relations, for instance, became less transparent when labor hiring agencies or other third parties were contracted to assign to suppliers a certain number of workers, who were then assigned to factories that had contracts with several different global brands.

The scale of the increasing concentration and rationalization of manufacturing in the readymade apparel sector, for instance, in different regions or countries was also influenced by trade agreements and relationships. Between 1989 and 2010 the apparel from China imported to the United States went from representing 13.55 percent of all apparel imported to 41.97 percent.[7] The admission of China into the World Trade Organization in 2001 also proved to have a significant influence in this rapid increase, but the trend would continue to be reflected as apparel production shifted to countries like Bangladesh, Cambodia, and Vietnam, where labor costs were even lower.[8]

The globalized system of manufacturing, production, and service delivery that now exists and is part of the global supply chain network for most companies presents a unique set of challenges for the faith-based investor who is concerned about human dignity and human rights. It often requires a due diligence across all the supply chain, from the point of acquiring the raw materials and capital to organize and operate a business, to the production and manufacturing process, and to the transportation and delivery of the product to the customer. Furthermore, it requires an assessment of how individual corporations or brands are not a part of the race to the bottom when they search for business opportunities but make good faith efforts to follow their human rights policies wherever they operate.

---

7. See US Department of Commerce, Office of Textiles and Apparel, *http://otexa.ita.doc.gov*, as cited in Mark Anner, Jennifer Bair, and Jeremy Blasi, "Buyer Power, Pricing Practices, and Labor Outcomes in Global Supply Chains," working paper, IBS, University of Colorado at Boulder, August 2012, page 6, accessed August 7, 2019, *https://wsr-network.org/wp-content/uploads/2018/02/inst2012-0011.pdf*.

8. Vikas Bajaj, "Bangladesh, With Low Pay, Moves In on China," *New York Times*, July 16, 2010, accessed August 7, 2019, *https://www.nytimes.com/2010/07/17/business/global/17textile.html*.

Protecting Human Dignity and Human Rights in the Twenty-First Century

Socially responsible investing especially protecting human dignity and promoting human rights remains an important challenge and opportunity for faith-based investors and for the institutions within their various faith traditions. The challenge is simply characterized by the changing circumstances in the manufacturing, commercial, and financial sectors as they have become more global and powerful and their networks of operation have grown increasingly complex, especially their networks of contractual relationships with suppliers and partners. The opportunity for increased due diligence is found through the many organizations, tools, and advances in technology that have resulted in improving transparency and metrics for measuring accountability.

In the last quarter of the twentieth century, multinational corporations searched for new sources of cheap labor in different regions of the world. These arrangements were aided by bilateral trade agreements that facilitated the movement of goods and capital to neighboring or strategically located countries or regions in order to meet their need for a stable and plentiful local workforce.

Export processing zones, free trade, and industrial zones were established by local governments to create jobs for their citizens and to accommodate the needs of various corporations. The establishment of the Maquiladora sector in a ten-mile section of northern Mexico allowed numerous corporations to ship parts across the United States border into Mexico, have their products assembled in newly constructed factories, and then ship them back across the same border for sale.

The commitment of faith-based and responsible investors has also been elevated because of the questions that have been raised by local congregations, social justice teams, and participants in their funds. The advances in reliable data gathering have allowed them to more easily identify many of the companies, suppliers, and specific factories that are being used for sourcing products. They have also been successful in building out broader interfaith and other networks of investors to address company managers and boards of directors. These engagements have resulted in putting corporations on notice that their operations in nearly every region of the world are being monitored and that investors and other stakeholders are including this information in evaluating the social and citizenship responsibility of a particular company and their decisions about including the company in their portfolios.

Resources and Tools Available to Faith-Based Investors Today

The resources, services, and tools available to investors who have made protecting human dignity and human rights a priority in their approach to investments have increased significantly over the years. Active shareholders were ready and willing to be attentive to the accounts of abuses that were raised in the media or in reports that they had received through their church and civil society networks, and they devoted significant resources to these engagement efforts.

The initial responses of companies who were questioned about any abuses in their factories either domestically or internationally were very limited, with a great deal of resistance to share too much information. Over time, as they assessed the validity of the questions that were being raised by shareholders, they did agree to invite shareholders to visit their operations in these zones and began to make some limited statements about how they were addressing the issues of concern, many of them about working conditions and the rights of workers.

These first steps by companies and investors were helpful but left several glaring gaps that were open to criticism. Investors did not have the resources or the organizational capacity to address the scale of the operations that an individual company or brand might have across different countries, and there was little or no third-party verification of the reports the companies produced. This concern was eventually addressed when third-party monitoring organizations were established and accepted by all parties. The emergence and expansion of social and environmental research firms that were employed by investors to collect and analyze information about the companies that were in their portfolios or companies that they were considering for investment significantly increased the quality of the due diligence available for responsible investors.

A second important contribution to this call for greater accountability and transparency was the emergence of several multistakeholder organizations that were concerned about protecting human rights and especially the rights of workers. They employed a combination of informed customers, civil society groups, and investors to organize and demand assurances that no child labor or abusive labor practices were used in the factories where products were made. One example is the Clean Clothes Campaign (www. cleanclothes.org) that was formed in the Netherlands in 1989 and has grown to be the largest alliance of labor unions and non-governmental organizations, with a partner network of over 250 organizations around the world. Their mission, which is to improve the working conditions in the garment and sportswear industries around the world, offered an immediate ally whose goals connected well with the mission of many faith-based investors and remains an invaluable information and strategy resource.

Another similar type of campaign is the International Cotton Campaign (www.cottoncampaign.org), which is focused on eliminating child labor and forced labor in the cotton fields of eighteen different countries, especially Turkmenistan and Uzbekistan where the abuses are orchestrated by the government. Like the Clean Clothes Campaign but with a focus on cotton production, this organization offers a trove of information to any investors who are interested in making these issues a priority in their investment policies.

The Kimberley Process (www.kimberleyprocess.com), which is focused on the diamond mining and delivery system, was launched in 2000 to reduce the flow of *conflict diamonds*—"rough diamonds used to finance wars against governments"—around the world. It was endorsed by the UN General Assembly in 2004, is backed by leading civil society organizations, and works with eighty-two countries. Some individual jewelry companies that have been active supporters of this process have also decided to include further benchmarks to ensure that their products carry additional certification assurances.

UN-Sponsored Initiatives and Sovereign Legislation

On a much broader scale, the UN Global Compact (www.unglobalcompact. org) is a nonbinding UN pact that was organized in 2000 to encourage businesses worldwide to adopt sustainable and socially responsible standards and to report on how they are implementing those standards. This represents a very large-scale global effort with over 9,500 companies based in 160 different countries, and includes collaboration with UN agencies, labor groups, and civil society. Monitoring compliance with the responsibilities of membership is a key factor for the successful advancement of the goals of the compact.

At the request of the UN secretary general, a group of the world's largest institutional investors initiated a process that led to the development of the Principles for Responsible Investment (www.unpri.org). The UN PRI was formally launched in April 2006. With over 2,000 members, the majority of whom are asset owners, UN PRI is an invaluable resource to help investors to engage corporations for research, networking, and collaboration with other institutional investors. As has been previously discussed in this chapter, the adoption of the United Nations Guiding Principles on Business and Human Rights (UNGPs) in 2011 also elaborated a very specific set of duties that governments and businesses must follow to protect human rights.

The UK Modern Slavery Act is an example of legislation in a sovereign jurisdiction that gives law enforcement officials the tools to fight modern slavery, to hold perpetrators accountable, and to support and protect victims. Under the French Duty of Care Law in 2017, certain large companies are under an affirmative obligation to prevent human rights violations. This legislation applies both within the company itself and to its subsidiaries, subcontractors, and suppliers.

Many other initiatives have been undertaken by collaborations of investors, civil society, and NGOs, each with a very specific mission to address abuses of human dignity and human rights. Some of these are focused on addressing abuses in a specific country or a specific industry, like the recently announced initiative asking for an independent commission to monitor the quality of tailings dams, a tool used in the mining industry. Others are focused on the human rights abuses in the agriculture and seasonal harvesting industries in developed and developing countries, or on the dangers to workers' health and safety—and eventually the health and safety of customers—from possible exposure to toxic chemicals used in the manufacturing process and embedded in the final product.

Conclusion

As faith-based investors seek to better align the management of their personal and institutional assets with their beliefs and with how those beliefs are expressed in the mission to promote human dignity and protect human rights, the history and the practices discussed in this chapter will hopefully serve as an inspiration and a guide. The many resources and tools that have been developed to bring the realization of this vision within reach continue to be improved and made more accessible. With the support of formal sectors like the United Nations and the conviction of many in the business community that their brands and their companies should protect human rights and promote human dignity, the future for advancing this campaign indeed looks promising.

Chapter 7

Investor Action on Climate Change*

*Patricia Daly and Tim Brennan***

This chapter tells the story of how faith-based investors have used their investments in shares of companies to give voice to concerns about climate change and to move companies to take positive action. Pension funds, pooled investment funds, denominational foundations, and Roman Catholic orders of sisters, brothers, and priests have been addressing climate change through their investments for decades. By acting together, these investors have been able to motivate companies to improve their disclosure, policies, and practices on climate change and to awaken other major investors to the risks of climate change.

Generally, shareholder actions are only available to those who hold individual securities, not mutual funds or other pooled vehicles. However, parishes, congregations, and individuals can encourage and foster the work of these larger funds by supporting their denominations' and diocesan or judicatory efforts and, where possible, by investing in these pooled funds. They can also choose mutual funds that are supportive of shareholder action and may collaborate with organizations of faith-based partnerships. As a tool for reflection, this chapter seeks to educate its readers on the work accomplished and what might be done in the future.

Owning stock in a company not only gives shareholders a financial interest in the profits (and losses) of a company, but a voice in how the company is governed and managed. It is "owning," after all, and there are rights and

---

* This material, including organizations and websites noted, is provided for informational purposes only and should not be viewed as an endorsement or as investment, tax, or other professional advice.

** Editor's note: This chapter is very much a history of an important issue (many would say the most important issue so as to ensure that the planet itself can continue to support and foster human and other life), with a focus on the progress made through engagements with companies through the efforts of many people involved with the ICCR. This continues to be an area where direct engagement with companies is crucial. Due to its importance, some religious investors retain direct ownership in certain fossil fuel companies specifically to encourage dialogue and change. As you will see in certain case studies in this book, some advocates of complete divestment of fossil fuel companies believe corporate engagement will not bring about the needed changes. However, we share this very personal reflection to demonstrate what has already been accomplished through collaboration and decisive action over time.

responsibilities to ownership. Faith-based investors engage with the companies they own in multiple ways and for multiple reasons. Through their ownership rights they may bring a moral, or values-based, message, speaking truth to power. And they do this because it is effective in changing the policies and practices of large corporate actors, thereby improving the lives of people and the care for the planet.

For several decades, religious investors have been pressing corporations to act to address climate change. Most notably, they have done this through shareholder resolutions published in the company's proxy statement and presented at the annual general meeting before the board, top management, and fellow shareholders. Less known, but no less important, are the ways in which shareholders have pressed companies through joint letters, conferences, and dialogue. While some are critical of shareholder engagement because they think it is not forceful enough, the evidence shows that it is effective.

How does shareholder advocacy work? (See chapter 4.) A shareholder has a platform from which to speak, which is different from social justice advocates and other stakeholders. This is because corporate boards and management have a common interest with shareholders in the long-term success of the company. This creates an opportunity to have a constructive exchange about what is truly in the long-term interest of the company and how considering its effects on the environment and communities can actually make the company better positioned for long-term sustainability.

The Emergence of Climate Change as an Investor Issue

In the late 1970s, the various interfaith communities in the United States and beyond integrated environmental concerns to their institutional attention. Several faith communities began to articulate their ecological concerns, as most realized that the 13.8 billon years of the universe and the 4.54 billion-year journey of Earth were God's first scriptures! Many investment guidelines for faith-based institutions were revised to include ecological concerns. The Eco-Justice Working Group of the National Council of Churches was formed during this time, with the World Council of Churches taking on environmental justice in 1991. Thanks to the initiative of the Presbyterian Church, the American Baptist Home Mission Society, and some Roman Catholic Orders, by the late 1980s climate change had become a pressing issue for many people of faith and was a focus of the UN Rio Earth Summit in 1992.

As many insurance companies reported that significant reserves had declined throughout the 1980s due to severe weather events, faith-based investors began to study the issue, reaching out to scientists and environmental groups. In studying global warming, they realized that severe climatic events would be far more dramatic in the developing world and cause far more suffering there. People who didn't have a concept of insurance were going to be most impacted while contributing little to nothing of the greenhouse gases (GHGs) that were causing the damage. Faith-based investors also understood that Creation itself, God's first scriptures, was being violated. Even the worst-case scenarios that were put forth at that time have since come to pass.[1]

One of the most prevalent organizations for faith-based investors is the Interfaith Center on Corporate Responsibility (ICCR), and the authors of this chapter have been directly involved in many of their efforts over several years. ICCR's first resolutions with the utility sector never mentioned global warming. Due to the oil shortages of the early 1970s, reducing energy use had become a common goal. ICCR asked the companies to report on their efforts to improve energy efficiency, especially demand-side management (DSM), a program that incentivized efficiencies and enabled customers to better understand and control their energy use.

Thanks to very effective marketing in the 1970s and 1980s, sales of minivans and SUVs took off. People in the United States were convinced that they needed large, gas-guzzling cars; the profit margin happened to be huge too. So ICCR first asked the auto companies to report on fuel efficiency.

Resolutions at the oil and gas companies first asked for a board review of the impact of global warming on the company, especially financially. Investor groups then moved on to asking the companies to report on their emissions.

Throughout the decades during which the faith-based investors brought concerns about global warming to companies, requests evolved. In the early 1990s, faith-based investors started with requests for efficiencies and soon asked for disclosure of GHG emissions. Today, most Fortune 500 companies report on their GHG emissions. Companies were also asked to report on their climate risk—that is, to explain what a company has in place when new technologies allow for a quick transition to alternatives, and when domestic and international policies limit emissions. Investors looked for climate

---

1. "Insurance Industry's Share of Weather-Related Losses Rising, Researcher Says," *Insurance Journal,* August 22, 2005, *https://www.insurancejournal.com/magazines/mag-features/2005/08/22/150532.htm.*

science expertise on boards of directors and asked companies to report on their investment in renewable energy and on their lobbying, political contributions, and support for industry groups that may mislead voters on global warming. Resolutions next asked companies to set GHG emissions reduction targets, and then, once the Paris Agreement was in place, to report on how the company would operate in a world where global temperature increases are limited to 2 degrees Celsius, the goal of the Paris Agreement.[2] This is often referred to as "two-degree scenario planning."

During the 1990s into the 2000s, many of these resolutions were supported by faith-based institutional investors and other supportive investors. Initially, those investors were happy to receive enough of a vote to be able to refile the resolution the following year.[3] By the early 2000s, large investors such as city and state pension funds realized the financial risk of global warming and began to support various resolutions.

Large Institutional Investors Awaken to Climate Change Risk

In 2002, Ceres (then called the Coalition for Environmentally Responsible Economies) issued a report entitled "Value at Risk: Climate Change and the Future of Governance"[4] with the endorsement of investors holding $300 billion in assets.[5] The report made the case that climate change presented multiple risks to company value and therefore needed to be addressed by boards of directors as a matter of fiduciary duty. The headline on CSRwire read, "Investor Coalition Finds U.S. Corporations Face Multi-Billion Dollar Risk from Climate Change."[6] Ceres had provided a solid business case for the necessity of companies

---

2. "The Paris Agreement," United Nations Climate Change, accessed May 27, 2019, *https://unfccc.int/process-and-meetings/the-paris-agreement/the-paris-agreement*.

3. "Shareholder Resolutions," The Forum for Sustainable and Responsible Investment, accessed September 9, 2019, *https://www.ussif.org/resolutions#targetText=To%20resubmit%20resolutions%20in%20subsequent, year%20and%20all%20years%20thereafter*. (SEC regulations, as of the writing of this book, allow companies to exclude resolutions where shareholder support does not exceed 3 percent in the first year, 6 percent in the second year, and 10 percent thereafter.)

4. "Value at Risk: Climate Change and the Future of Governance," Ceres, April 30, 2002, *https://www.ceres.org/resources/reports/value-risk-climate-change-and-future-governance*.

5. "Ceres' Sustainable Governance Project Releases Major Climate Change Report," Trillium Asset Management, May 1, 2002, *https://trilliuminvest.com/ceres-sustainable-governance-project-releases-major-climate-change-report/*.

6. "Investor Coalition Finds U.S. Corporations Face Multi-Billion Dollar Risk from Climate Change," CSRwire, April 18, 2002, *http://www.csrwire.com/press_releases/23386-Investor-Coalition-Finds-U-S-Corporations-Face-Multi-Billion-Dollar-Risk-from-Climate-Change*.

addressing climate change, enhancing the climate risk concerns already in play by the faith-based investors in addition to the moral case for action.

In early 2003, Ceres, in partnership with the UN Foundation, organized the first Investor Summit on Climate Risk at the United Nations. The meeting was strategically scheduled the day after the annual conference of the National Association of State Treasurers, which was taking place in New York City. Treasurers have key roles in overseeing state pension funds in most states. Ceres saw this as an opportunity to deliver the message of climate change as a risk to shareholder value to an audience that could be influential, with pension funds holding billions of dollars in assets. Initially, most of these treasurers were somewhat perplexed by the invitation they received from Kofi Annan, secretary general of the United Nations at the time. Many invitees may have asked themselves the same question as the companies: "Climate change may be a risk, but it's a matter of public policy; what does it have to do with me?" But many of them came to the meeting regardless. And what they heard began to change the tide. At that meeting a core of investors with assets under management (AUM) of $1 trillion issued a call for action by investors. That was a beginning.[7]

In the years since, the message that climate change presents a bevy of risks to companies and to investment portfolios has been taken up by a growing number of investors. These risks include physical risk to assets and infrastructure; regulatory risk, both actual and anticipated; and stranded asset risk from assets and technologies that become obsolete. The Investor Summit has convened biennially since 2003, each year with more assets under management represented than the year before. The 2018 summit was attended by investors with $30 trillion in AUM. That's 30 times the AUM that endorsed the 2003 statement.[8] During the same period, Ceres organized the Ceres Investor Network on Climate Risk and Sustainability (previously INCRS), which now comprises 168 institutional investors, collectively managing more than $26 trillion in assets.[9]

Meanwhile, faith-based investors continued to lead shareholder engagements on climate change, drawing on their deep and long-term business

---

7. "Investors Want Wall Street Climate Info," CNN, November 24, 2003, accessed July 28, 2019, *http://www.cnn.com/2003/TECH/science/11/24/climate.finances.reut/index.html.*

8. "Summit Draws Major Investors with $30 Trillion in AUM to Map Out Next Steps Tackling Climate Risk and Seizing Low-Carbon Opportunities," Ceres, January 31, 2018, accessed August 4, 2019 *https://www.ceres.org/news-center/press-releases/summit-draws-major-investors-30-trillion-aum-map-out-next-steps-tackling.*

9. "Ceres Investor Network on Climate Risk and Sustainability," Ceres, accessed May 19, 2019, *https://www.ceres.org/networks/ceres-investor-network.*

relationships with company executives. While their assets under management were now dwarfed by the pension funds and asset managers in the INCRS, they played a major role in filing resolutions and leading dialogues with companies.

It might be surprising to learn that shareholder-initiated resolutions rarely receive majority votes. Then, how can they be effective? It's important to understand that many of the shares are held by the company or by individuals and institutions closely tied to the company.

It is not uncommon for shares, particularly those controlled by brokers, to be reflexively voted in line with management recommendations. Thus, while it varies from one company to another, anywhere from 20 to 50 percent of shares are not actually in play. In almost all cases, those who vote *for* these shareholder resolutions are voting *against* management. The corporate executives know this math, and they sit up and take notice when significant numbers of shareholders vote against their recommendations, even if it is less than a majority. The truism seems to be that a resolution gets the attention of the board once it receives 10 percent of the vote, indicating this concern will not go away. For some companies, it may be that the new resolutions, including those put forward by faith-based investors, are the canary in the coal mine and get special attention because the concern will be front and center within five years, and they may as well get ahead of the issue.

Shareholder resolutions are not one-off events, and this is very true for resolutions relating to climate action. They are typically multiyear campaigns with a goal of building support year after year. Votes are heavily influenced by the recommendations of the proxy voting advisors. These advisors typically withhold support for new resolutions until they get a sense of how shareholders view them. When a new proposal gets significant shareholder support, say 10 to 15 percent, the proxy advisors take a closer look and may change their recommendation. Then if a proposal earns growing support over a number of years, increasing to 20 to 30 percent, management knows that major institutional investors are voting against them, and they take notice. Furthermore, top management and boards do not like these issues being raised at the annual general meeting of the company, especially when they have to announce that 20, 30, or 40 percent have voted against their recommendations.

In 2018 and 2019 we have witnessed a shift in some of this behavior as one or more of the proxy voting advisors, and some of the largest investment firms, have supported first-time resolutions on human rights resolutions related to gun safety, new facial recognition technologies aimed at immigrants, and child exploitation through social media. It appears that there is a serious shift occurring among a larger group of investors to support broader social justice issues.

Very often, rising support leads a company to agree to a dialogue. This is the real goal of shareholders: not to make a scene at the annual meeting, but to have a substantive discussion about the issues in a meeting with top management who have expertise and control over the issue. When these dialogues are conducted in good faith with informed shareholders and open-minded management, real progress can be made.

According to ISS Analytics:

> The last decade saw a dramatic change in investors' attitudes towards environmental and social issues. A confluence of factors has led to the increase in the median level of support for environmental and social shareholder proposals as a percentage of votes cast from the middle single digits from 2000 until 2008 to the 24 percent in 2018, including pressures from the public and regulators in the aftermath of the financial crisis, global policy initiatives, major disaster events, and *the evolution of the debate by proponents from a values-based framework to a value-oriented discussion of managing potential business risks.* Increasingly, investors embraced sustainability and became more actively engaged on the issues.[10]

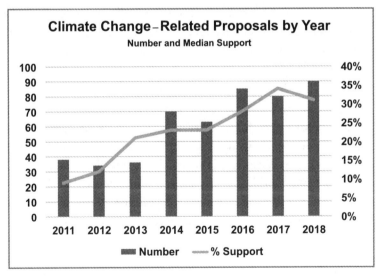

Source: ISS Analytics

10. Kosmas Papadopoulos, "The Long View: US Proxy Voting Trends on E&S Issues from 2000 to 2018," ISS Analytics, January 31, 2019, *https://corpgov.law.harvard.edu/2019/01/31/the-long-view-us-proxy-voting-trends-on-es-issues-from-2000-to-2018/.* Emphasis added.

The Future of Engagement on Climate Change

So what are the priorities of faith-based and other values investors going forward? As has been true from the beginning, those working in this area bring focus to those most adversely affected by climate change and the efforts to address the problem—the poor and the marginalized. Here are some of the current priorities:

- There is growing interest in what is being called *Just Transition*: advocating for workers and communities that are adversely affected when a company takes steps to reduce emissions (for instance when a utility closes a coal-powered plant) and for those people and communities globally who have contributed the least to the causes of climate change but who are now, and will be, suffering the most. These are all hard choices and difficult issues to resolve equitably, involving redeploying workers and changing industries which have been significant employers in some areas for decades.

- Progress with positive environmental change has also been challenged by lobbying and election spending that is inhibiting strong policy action on climate change.

- Pressing companies to produce two-degree scenario reports is a major priority following on the successes at several oil companies. Investors are asking companies to produce reports that are prepared in line with the recommendations of the Task Force on Climate-Related Financial Disclosures, or TCFD.[11] Having a standard framework for disclosure is very important in order that the reports are comprehensive and comparable.

- Following on the United Nations' Intergovernmental Panel on Climate Change report in the fall of 2018, investors are now saying that the 2 degree Celsius target is not enough. The report showed that the damage from a rise of 2 degrees Celsius will be extensive, and that prudence would have the world targeting a maximum increase of 1.5 degrees.[12] We recognize that this is extremely ambitious, and that many believe that even limiting the increase to 2 degrees is not possible.

---

11. Task Force on Climate-Related Financial Disclosures, accessed May 19, 2019, *https://www.fsb-tcfd. org/*.

12. "Summary for Policymakers of IPCC Special Report on Global Warming of 1.5°C Approved by Governments," Intergovernmental Panel on Climate Change, October 8, 2018, accessed August 4, 2019, *https://www.ipcc.ch/2018/10/08/summary-for-policymakers-of-ipcc-special-report-on-global-warming-of-1-5c-approved-by-governments/*.

Because of a strategic decision to remain directly engaged and to be able to vote and make proposals to company management, many faith-based investors have chosen to retain their direct ownership in the shares of companies that are major emitters of greenhouse gasses, including utilities, producers and transmitters of oil and gas, the auto sector, airlines, and industrial manufacturers. There may be investment reasons to do this, but more importantly it gives investors who feel a sacred obligation to Creation and people whose voices have been marginalized a seat at the table. When investors do not hold stock directly, that voice is absent, and the company can be much less responsive regarding climate change issues. When religious entities can hold stock directly, it is essential that investors with faith and values be in a position to use their ownership rights to hold companies accountable. However, this has been and will continue to be complicated work, better undertaken when done through collaboration with others. For those who hold their assets through secular funds and denominational investment vehicles, encouraging the entities holding those stocks directly to engage with organizations taking collaborative action is also a way to remain engaged. Please see chapter 9 for a way that some entities could hold stocks directly for this purpose, without committing their endowment assets, if the congregation/organization did not wish to do that.

Responsible shareholders continue to work with companies on the new challenges related to climate change. But we are faced with a profound transition in how energy must be produced. Those solutions aren't clear yet. Some renewable energy initiatives have become very affordable, but the transition needed to keep us below 2 degrees Celsius will take massive investment. Many Europeans and their institutions have taken the lead in this. There are some efforts in the United States and other regions, but the magnitude of the effort demands a major shift in investment priorities that cannot be the focus of this book. There are several fossil-free investment products, but, in the opinion of this chapter's authors, these will never get us to where we need to be. Focused investment on clean energy, either through direct ownership or through funds, should be part of everyone's portfolio and be present on the minds of all of our leaders.

In addition, some congregations and organizations have also worked with their own local or national denominational entities to investigate how they could reduce use of fossil fuels, and have also gotten involved in various environmental initiatives. Please reach out to your denomination or local judicatory for leads on how your congregation/organization could get involved in environmental efforts in addition to direct investing.

Chapter 8

Creating Positive Change: Impact Investing, Community Development, and the Rethinking of Returns*

Mark A. Regier

Truly I tell you, whatever you did for one of the least of these brothers and sisters of mine, you did for me. (Matt. 25:40, NIV)

In previous chapters, you have had the opportunity to explore some of the many ways faith-driven investors can impact our world and its people for the better. For most of these strategies, the focus is on either limiting the negative or leveraging the positive influence of our existing capital, using the traditional tools and mechanisms of the investment industry. And, as you have read, the real-world impact can be amazing!

There are, however, another set of faith-based investing options that start *first* with the needs of vulnerable communities and environments in their drive to create positive change. This rapidly expanding pool of change-oriented products and strategies has roots extending back as far as any of those that have been reviewed to this point. *Impact investing*—traditionally known as community development or high social impact investing—grew organically from relationships that many congregations, parachurch organizations, and denominational agencies had with local, underserved communities and ministries around the world.

What distinguished these investment opportunities from others in the socially responsible investing pantheon was not only their deep grassroots' connections, but also the willingness of investors to value the desired social or environmental outcome equal to or higher than the financial return in the

---

* This material, including organizations and websites noted, is provided for informational purposes only and should not be viewed as an endorsement or as investment, tax, or other professional advice.

investment's evaluation. Social impact wasn't just a side benefit of the investment; it was the goal. This led many in the investment industry to label these investments as "below-market" or "concessionary." This also meant that many, even religious, institutional investors did not—or could not—find a place for them in their portfolios.

My own organization has been involved with impact or community development investing strategies for nearly three decades. This work has been both natural—for an organization committed to integrating faith and finances from a biblical perspective of Christian stewardship—but also challenging—for a financial institution whose primary fiduciary responsibility is the management of invested assets belonging to others.

Fortunately, the field of impact investing has grown and evolved dramatically over the past ten years and now encompasses a wide range of investment structures and financial risk and return parameters. Today, there is literally "something for everyone" seeking to make a targeted impact through their investment portfolio.

However, the place to begin should not be what you want (or even need) by way of financial returns, but rather in forming a firm understanding of the role faith plays in your investment decisions—including the degree to which you might deliberately consider investments in those living on the social and economic margins of our society.

The Biblical Foundation for Change through Investment

My organization, the Mennonite Foundation/Everence Financial Ministries of the Mennonite Church USA, has long viewed our work—helping individuals, organizations, and congregations integrate their faith and finances—through an Anabaptist understanding of scripture. This perspective suggests to us that some of the most important teachings related to money and finances don't reference these topics directly.

As we consider how investing can help shape the world around us, in a way that is pleasing to God and responsible to those around us, we're challenged to reflect on both the "vertical" and "horizontal" natures of our faith.

The vertical dimension concerns our direct relationship with God—our desire to reflect God's values in our worship, our thoughts, our prayers, and our deeds. The horizontal aspect reflects our relationship with the individuals and communities around us, including our relationship to Creation itself.

We see this clearly in Christ's response to a question about the greatest commandment, recorded in the Gospels of Matthew and Mark:

"The most important one," answered Jesus, "is this: 'Hear, O Israel: The Lord our God, the Lord is one. Love the Lord your God with all your heart and with all your soul and with all your mind and with all your strength.' The second is this: 'Love your neighbor as yourself.' There is no commandment greater than these." (Mark 12:29–31, NIV)

Historically, faithfulness on the vertical axis of our relationship to God has been measured through the purity of our choices, actions, and thoughts—often called "holiness." In the field of investing, holiness has often taken the form of avoidance. Religious organizations and individuals have long sought to reflect their faithfulness to God's values by the investments they've rejected.

And as our world—both socially and economically—has grown more complex, however, this approach to faithfulness has become an increasing challenge. As we address modern slavery found in conflict minerals inside every cellphone and laptop, or the sweatshops hidden behind our favorite clothing brands, or the racism and sexism that can lurk within even the most respected corporations, being pure is difficult (see chapters 5 and 6).

In addition, this vertical emphasis focuses on our own reflection of God's purity, potentially overlooking the horizontal call to love our neighbor and other aspects of God's Creation.

How, then, should we respond to the horizontal, reflecting the gift of life and grace from God? What is our response—through our investments—to repeated calls throughout scripture to care for the widow and orphan, protect the weak, and minister to the poor?

Just What Is Required?

This question (and answer) by an Old Testament prophet in Micah is fundamental to our fullest understanding of Christian discipleship. People of faith are called to "do justice, and to love kindness, and to walk humbly with your God" (Micah 6:8). Micah tells us that our actions and choices here on earth do matter—and we believe our investments do too.

This surprising message follows a series of questions about which offerings and sacrifices are required to bring restoration to the sinning, straying children of Israel. The questions betray a misunderstanding of God's larger purpose, focusing on pursuing the correct ritual for the situation instead of striving for justice and kindness as part of our interactions with others.

Many Christians have taken this call seriously—looking to their faith as a guide for their charitable giving, support for missions, choice of vocation, and the ways they relate to their families and local communities. Far fewer, however, have explored how this call to justice, kindness, and a humble walk with God impacts their investment portfolio.

A Lesson from the Good Samaritan

If God's values and concerns are the objective of our investing witness, how do we measure and manage the impact our investments are having?

Authentic Christian faith requires engagement in the world, with all of its contradictions and nuances. What better example of a person trying to live faithfully in a heated political and religious setting than the Samaritan in Jesus's familiar parable?

This parable was offered in response to a question posed to Jesus, asking, "And who is my neighbor?" It again focuses on the horizontal axis ("others") of our relationship with God. And it is a question that remains as important today as it was then.

Found in Luke 10:25–37, this story—in its simplest form—has been baked into American culture. Many, regardless of religious background, will recognize the story of the virtuous man who helped a person in need while others passed by.

In short, the Samaritan, from an ethnic group scorned by the culture of Jesus's audience, stopped to help a man wounded by robbers while a priest and a Levite passed him by. These holy men presumably continued on their way because touching the wounded man would have made them unclean, according to the religious rules of the day.

When Jesus flipped a question back to the questioner, asking, "Which of these three . . . was a neighbor to the man who fell into the hands of the robbers?" the answer was obvious: "The one who showed him mercy" (Luke 10:36–37). Jesus emphasized the horizontal relationship between fellow travelers despite their different ethnicities and beliefs, and by doing so, admonished the characters who placed a higher value on their narrow understanding of what was expected of them.

We could replace any of these characters with modern stand-ins and get a similar reflective opportunity. The call, then, is to self-sacrificial action on behalf of the disadvantaged or vulnerable—a message repeated frequently throughout the New Testament. It would seem credible that a similar approach could be applied to at least a part of a mission-oriented portfolio.

With more than 2,350 references in the Bible to money and resource-related issues, it seems clear that the writers and the early church understood the power and importance of the financial aspects of our lives. And while the financial tools of our society differ greatly from those of the first century, many of the challenges remain the same.

As you have already read about the potential for change through share-holder advocacy and proxy voting (see chapter 4), a closer look at the lens and history of impact investing will demonstrate the opportunities available for serving both God and neighbor in entirely new ways.

The Local Lens of Real-World Transformation

Almost all faith communities and ministries are essentially "local" in nature. They exist to connect individuals to one another and the higher purpose and divine presence of our Christian faith. From the very beginning Christians sought to follow the teachings of Christ in a real and meaningful way, one that addressed the needs of the communities they inhabited and the people they met.

Whether through Paul's challenge to the early church on being generous to the historic role Roman Catholic orders have played in bringing education and medicine to the needy, or the innumerable Christian ministries founded to meet both physical and spiritual needs, the Church has sought to be real and relevant on a local level throughout the ages.

Over two millennia of service and ministry have given the faith community a deep—if far from perfect—connection to the hurts, needs, and wants of societies around the globe. This work has led and continues to lead us to ever better, bolder efforts to meet our fellow humans where they are, as they are, responding to the light of God's presence we already see in them. It is an engagement that is real, personal, and challenging in many ways.

It should be no surprise, then, that people of faith have been at the forefront of the field we now know as "community development" since the phrase was coined. Understanding human and community needs, shaping responses, and building missing infrastructure have given us a unique lens with which to understand both the demands and opportunities of real-world transformation. Frequently, the faith community has responded to these needs through charitable activities and institution building.

Only recently—within the past fifty years or so—has the faith community begun to understand that this same real-world, transformational lens can be applied to the investment arena. And, once again, early faith-based pioneers in this work have laid the foundation of much of what we see today in impact investing.

A History of Its Own

Amid the history of the growth of the socially responsible investing movement covered elsewhere in this book, the evolution of impact investing deserves some attention in its own right. Fortunately, the rise and impact of community development financial institutions (CDFIs)—financial institutions that are 100 percent dedicated to delivering responsible, affordable lending to low-income, low-wealth, and other disadvantaged people—has been exhaustively documented in a recent book by Clifford N. Rosenthal, *Democratizing Finance: Origins of the Community Development Financial Institutions Movement*. And Rosenthal should know—he's been there from the movement's beginning in 1980. He documents how faith-motivated investors and community organizations, along with broader social change movements of the day, aligned to give birth to an entire financial services subsector, dedicated to sustainably opening doors of economic opportunity for disadvantaged individuals and communities.[1]

Noteworthy is the emergence of three key categories of CDFIs—community development credit unions, community development banks, and community development loan funds. Each of these categories has grown into subindustries with unique roles and contributions, along with their own trade associations. They provide a broad range of products and services for both mission-driven investors and underserved communities. I provide additional detail on each of these categories later in this chapter.

It is important to note that with the rise of community development investing (now impact investing), in many cases it was faith-based institutions and organizations—particularly Roman Catholic orders of religious

---

1. Clifford N. Rosenthal, *Democratizing Finance: Origins of the Community Development Financial Institutions Movement* (Victoria, BC: FriensenPress, 2018).

women—that made early investments in these CDFIs, even to the point of suffering financial losses. Their decision to place mission alignment, viewed through the local lens of transformation, above financial return on a portion of their portfolio made them the "capital catalysts" of the day. Their willingness to accept lower-than-market-rate returns (as viewed from a traditional risk-return analysis) helped develop new models of low-income finance, combined with necessary borrower technical assistance and support, that have proven to be both stable and successful over the long term.

While in the intervening years the impact investing energy and headlines have been focused elsewhere, prominent philanthropic investors along with family offices (professional investment firms that manage the personal and charitable investments of one or more high net worth families) and others have, today, begun to return to the important role of concessionary community investing. They bring a renewed understanding of the critical role this form of "catalytic capital" plays in the broader community development economic ecosystem by funding critical or priming initiatives necessary for future growth. Their efforts are helping to bring new attention, investment, and analysis to this important capital stream at a scale the faith community could never deliver on its own.

Finally, a historical review of the evolution of impact investing would not be complete without a discussion of the emergence, over the last decade, of a new class of investments designed to integrate targeted social and environmental impact with more risk-adjusted financial returns. The Rockefeller Foundation is credited with coining the term "impact investing" in 2007 during a gathering of socially oriented investors seeking to broaden and define the range of high social impact investments available to philanthropic and mission-driven organizations. Today this spectrum includes high-risk PRIs (program related investments), traditional concessionary community investments, federally insured deposits in community development banks and credit unions, microfinance investments, green real estate, social venture capital, and more, each offering a unique mix of social impact and risk-adjusted returns.[2]

The field and opportunities for impact investing have become worldwide. The Global Impact Investing Network (GIIN, www.thegiin.org) has emerged to help give structure and connection to this rapidly expanding investment

---

2. Saadia Madsbjerg, "Bringing Scale to the Impact Investing Industry," Rockefeller Foundation, August 15, 2018, accessed August 4, 2019, *https://www.rockefellerfoundation.org/blog/bringing-scale-impact-investing-industry/*.

universe, linking philanthropic, socially responsible, and faith-based investors in their quest to make a lasting difference through their portfolios.

Impact Investing Opportunities for All

The most exciting aspect of this stage of impact investing's journey is the explosive growth we have seen—and will continue to see—in investment options and vehicles. Today, there is quite literally something for every risk appetite, return hurdle, or impact priority, with more on the way. Below, I offer a brief overview of the various impact investing categories available to investors, along with industry organizations and websites where you can learn more.

Community Development Credit Unions

Similar to traditional credit unions but chartered to serve specific disadvantaged communities or populations, these financial institutions are overseen and insured by NCUA (National Credit Union Administration, www.ncua.gov). They offer mission-driven depository products and banking services specially designed to meet the unique needs of their underserved target market. Inclusiv (www.inclusiv.org), formerly the National Federation of Community Development Credit Unions, provides industry support and services for CDCUs.

Community Development Banks

These are FDIC insured banking institutions with a primary mission of serving low- and moderate-income markets, working in urban and rural communities that lack access to credit and are not adequately served by the traditional banking industry. Like CDCUs, these banks offer products for mission-driven investors and banking services specifically tailored to their underserved communities. While the number of community development banks is relatively small, their impact is profound. The Community Development Bankers Association (www.cdbanks.org) is the organizing body for institutions in this field.

Community Development Loan Funds

These nonprofit lending institutions provide capital access to disadvantaged individuals and organizations with a degree of flexibility not found in regulated institutions, such as banks. Investment opportunities in such loan funds are primarily for accredited (or large, sophisticated) investors and can include equity investments, subordinated loans, and senior debt, all with commensurate degrees of risk and return. Opportunity Finance Network (www. ofn.org) is the industry association for community development loan funds.

Community or Impact Investing Intermediaries

These intermediaries serve to pool direct placements with other community development financial institutions, providing shared risk, professional due diligence, and security enhancements to benefit both individual and institutional investors.

Positive Impact Bonds

Positive impact bonds are socially or environmentally targeted, market rate fixed income investments issued by banks, multilateral institutions, corporations, states and municipalities, and other bond-issuing institutions (colleges, nonprofits, etc.). These targeted bonds are identified by a number of monikers—green bonds, social bonds, sustainability bonds, climate bonds, and others. And while such bonds are hard to access individually—they are frequently oversubscribed by multiples—such positive impact bonds can be found in leading, diversified fixed income funds. There is no central clearinghouse for these bond issues, but the Climate Bond Initiative (www.climate bonds.net), International Capital Market Association (www.icmagroup.org/green-social-and-sustainability-bonds/), and the World Bank (www.world bank.org) all have substantial information on green and sustainable bonds on their websites.

Targeted Public Equities

The issue of socially responsible public equities—or "stocks"—has been addressed previously in chapters on both screening and shareholder advocacy. However, in recent years, we've seen the emergence of equity mutual funds targeted at a specific social or environmental impact, delivered through the active management of the stock selection process. From gender lens investing to green energy and clean tech, targeted impact is being delivered. The Forum for Sustainable and Responsible Investment (USSIF, www.ussif.org)

is the industry trade association for socially responsible and ESG investing and a great place to start a search for such funds.

Social Venture Capital (SVC)

SVC provides an intersection between investor capital and the rapidly growing social entrepreneur movement. Clearly at the extreme end of the risk-return spectrum, social venture capital provides the potential of big social gains along with large financial returns—and surely a strong dose of risk! While not for the faint of heart, the possibilities for people, planet, and investors are powerful here. The Social Venture Circle (www.svcimpact.org) brings social entrepreneurs, impact investors, and capacity builders together to foster growth and development opportunities.

Grappling with the Issue of "Returns"

The most challenging issue for investors exploring the possibility of including impact investments in their portfolio is understanding how they—and/ or their advisors and consultants—should view the issue of "returns" for these investments.

For decades, faith-based investors have understood the concept of "returns" in a strictly financial sense. Whether out of faithfulness or fear, investment committees, church boards, organizational managers, and, particularly, investment consultants have decided to avoid the philosophical challenges and complexities of various faith-based investing strategies and just "earn as much as possible" for the good of the organization or individual. For some, their legal fiduciary duty precluded many of these options, but for far more it was deemed the prudent path, the path of least risk of recrimination.

As chapters throughout this book have described, things are quite different today—opening up new opportunities to invest with our faith values but without fear of critique. The mainstream investment industry's widespread adoption of the material aspects of environmental, social, and governance factors has brought a new level of respectability to SRI practices once considered "fringe." SRI and values-driven investment products are frequently competitive with other investments in both cost and long-term financial performance. The deep desire of millennials (and their boomer parents) to live and invest in alignment with their values—and see the institutions they support do the same—is pressing this change at a surprising pace.

But most importantly, these changes present the faith community—individuals and institutions alike—with a fresh opportunity to rethink their understanding of "returns" on their investments. How do we understand Christ's holistic call to steward God's resources—human and environmental as well as financial? What returns would God value? It's an opportunity to consider which of the many faith-based strategies an organization might try; to discuss what potential new efforts at mission-aligned investing might bring to an organization; and to value the commitment (itself an act of faithfulness) to at least ask the question "What might we do?" of managers, boards, vendors, advisors, and investment counselors.

For those looking for resources to help guide these conversations, check out the 1K Churches program of the Criterion Institute (www.criterion institute.org/our-work/congregations). This program helps congregations and organizations look deeply at the opportunity for using finance for social change and finding the solution(s) that are right for them.

Final Thoughts

The reality and opportunity set for each individual and organization will be different. And there is truly no "right answer." Rather, we have a calling in scripture—echoed by disadvantaged communities and even by Creation itself—to a conversation about the possibilities of using our God-given resources in a way that both respects the sacred fiscal duty we hold and responds to a world in need around us.

Faithfulness is not solely about the financial return on our portfolio, but in trusting that God will be with us on this stewardship journey.

Chapter 9

Inspiring Donors through Investing with Values*

James W. Murphy

Do not neglect to do good and to share what you have, for such sacrifices are pleasing to God. (Heb. 13:16)

Throughout this book (if you have not noticed yet), we are encouraging you to "do good" and take action, even if those next steps in your journey are small and incremental. Normally, when leaders are dealing with issues involving managing investments, including choices on socially responsible or environmental, social, and governance investing, the focus solely is on investment performance and ensuring proper management through diversification and strategic asset allocations, and the steady growth of those assets over time. That focus is very important for being a good fiduciary, but rarely do those activities cross over to the many considerations leaders should keep in mind for fundraising or "development" of new gifts to charitable institutions. However, this is yet another opportunity to do *good*.

This chapter will seek to educate you on that perspective as another consideration for steps taken around implementing SRI/ESG. Your incremental actions could actually inspire some people to give new gifts to your congregation or organization! In fact, I believe that your parish, agency, judicatory, or order is missing a tremendous opportunity if you do not seek to encourage more giving to your congregation/organization when taking these steps. As the members of the Episcopal Church Foundation team often say, "Good investment returns will grow your endowment/invested funds incrementally, but new planned and other special gifts will grow them exponentially!"

---

* This material, including organizations and websites noted, is provided for informational purposes only and should not be viewed as an endorsement or as investment, tax, or other professional advice.

Encouraging Giving

There have been many fine articles and books written on how to inspire donors to give generously to an organization. You may wish to review the many, many resources available through the Association of Fundraising Professionals (AFP) at www.afpglobal.org or other sources for more detailed assistance, or you may wish to seek the help of a professional fundraiser, or some of the denominational resources in the appendix of this book. Most of your denominations provide donor-giving and stewardship resources to guide leaders in various efforts, including many helpful yearlong plans. Those resources help foster individual generosity and turn people's hearts to support their congregations in giving more of their time, talent, and treasure. In our appendix of resources, please review the options from your denomination or denominational foundation, and also check out the many resources of the wonderful multidenominational organization, the Ecumenical Stewardship Center, at www.stewardshipresources.org. All of these resources will help you to engage in these vital efforts and teach you how to encourage your congregants/constituents to realize that all that we have and all that we are belongs to God, and we are merely stewards over all of it.

For this chapter, I will share with you thoughts and perspectives based on my experiences with primarily Episcopal Church entities: parishes, dioceses, schools, and various church agencies that support the numerous ministries of my (very) mainline denomination. I hope that most of my suggestions will apply in your circumstances as well. Without going into great detail on the technical aspects of gifts, please understand that when individuals make financial gifts to your congregation/organization, they typically make one of three kinds:

1. **Annual** gifts: normally from current income which, though typically unrestricted in purpose, may rise and fall with personal economic changes.

2. **Capital or major** gifts: from assets or pledged commitments paid over a period of time, usually for specifically defined projects, and often relying on a few large dollar gifts from wealthy individuals to support a large goal.

3. **Planned or estate/legacy** gifts: often the largest gift a committed donor will give, usually given at death through one's estate or assets held for retirement; normally the largest planned gifts come from people of perceived "average" means and not from the known-to-be-wealthy.

Each type of gift requires varying levels of cultivation and preparation. For example, it is much easier for a person to write a check or transfer stock than the more time-consuming efforts of including you in their estate plans with the help of legal professionals. Worry not, dear reader: there are many denominational and secular resources available to help you with all of these efforts.

New Opportunities

Nearly all denominations struggle with drawing in and retaining new members in our modern United States, where church attendance continues to decline. For most mainline denominations, decline in membership has been quite severe in recent decades, and well reported to leaders. (The reasons for that decline cannot be the focus of this reflection.) However, the overall decline of members does have a direct impact on giving to congregations and other religious organizations. In fact, more and more discussions are taking place (and thankfully some actions are actually being taken) to encourage congregations to diversify their "income streams" beyond a singular reliance on weekly congregational contributions.

Many mainline churches are being encouraged to do what several successful nonprofits have done: find new sources of revenue by coming up with new creative income opportunities. For most congregations, those are witnessed in rentals or other real-estate collaborations or opportunities, like leasing cell phone towers, and many other options. In addition, there is a renewed focus on growing endowments to much more substantial levels with new gifts, just as many universities are doing. Larger endowment funds afford reliable sources of income to fund and secure important ministries both now and in the future. In my own experience over the past twelve years, fewer congregations still fear that having larger endowments will have a detrimental impact on normal congregational giving. This is probably due to their witnessing that many nonprofits and colleges with tremendous endowments rarely have trouble raising regular annual gifts, while also conducting enormous capital campaigns.

I do not view this new development of seeking new income sources and new endowment gifts as negative, but actually as a tremendously positive change. I think this encourages congregations and church organizations to become even more directly engaged with the "real world" around them, as well as providing new opportunities for funding their good work. Changes like this are not a threat to the church—they just may be a new way for religious institutions to support themselves and their vital ministries beyond the collection plate. Not all readers will agree with me but, as I hope you read in this book's introduction, I don't think we all need to agree on everything to serve God and our fellow humans better.

Now more than ever, you as a leader of your congregation or religious organization should be concerned with how to grow your endowment, and other financial resources, with new gifts. You may not think of yourself as a fundraiser, and you may associate some negative views with that designation; or, possibly, you simply do not want to "ask someone for money." However, if you believe in the future mission and ministry of your congregation organization and wish to be a church leader serving the gospel's imperative to "go and make disciples," you will need financial resources to do that, in addition to the grace of God and the support of your community of faith. Again, worry not: your incremental and decisive actions will often speak "loudly" on your behalf, and inspire people to give. Or as has been attributed to that very great and quite radical medieval saint, Francis of Assisi, "Preach Jesus always, and if necessary, use words."

Inspiring Donors

Why might your work on SRI/ESG investing be a way to inspire new gifts to your endowment or other funds? Summarizing one of the most important aspects of fundraising, whether one is a volunteer or professional, fundraisers are seeking to match donor passions with philanthropic opportunities; this is one of the main roles of any fundraiser. Making your constituents aware of your congregation/organization's choice to pursue SRI/ESG through public meetings, online postings, and written updates (as was suggested in chapter 4) will inspire donors *if* you also note opportunities where individuals can support these efforts by making a gift. Demonstrating and publicizing an organization's choice to investigate and implement socially responsible investing may be an effective part of your efforts to raise funds for your organization, both from current gifts to an endowment and other funds, as well as through planned gifts from individual estates and retirement assets.

One of the best ways to inspire giving is by openly publicizing your endowment and investment policies. This can be done either directly on your website, or, whenever endowments or your investments are being discussed, by offering that those documents can be made available upon request. As previously reviewed in chapters 2 and 3, including what your congregation/ organization has decided to do regarding SRI/ESG in its investment policy statement (see sample IPSs in our appendix) will enable all constituents to witness the congregation/organization's commitment in this area. That alone may inspire giving.

Additionally, there may likely be potential donors who will be inspired to commit to making a current gift based on the congregation/organization's commitment to SRI, perhaps even to enable the entity to invest directly in stocks and participate in direct shareholder activism. To test that level of interest, when leaders are talking/blogging/writing about what is being done or being considered for SRI (see chapter 4), add a note or phrase that individual contributions may be made to support this effort. Also note that gifts could literally be used to enable ownership of specific stocks, if that is a choice your congregation/organization has made. Those particular donors may or may not wish their gift to become a part of your endowment, and your regular endowment policies may not even permit the holding of securities directly anyway, but that donor may wish their gift to make possible this special ministry at your congregation/organization.

However, even if that same donor indicates that they are only interested in making a current gift to sponsor this special work in some way, no good fundraiser (and I want to help you become one) would stop there and never inquire again. When the timing is right in the future, you could raise another possibility for those same individuals to give a more permanent gift. If it is within your organization's strategic vision and goals, you should be encouraging additional donations, possibly the setup of an endowment fund or other assets from those same donors who demonstrated those convictions earlier. Such fundraising is easier than you might have originally thought, as long as your lay and clergy leaders are regularly raising awareness to various constituents about your actions to implement your SRI/ESG work, and being transparent regarding all other financial matters.

The Importance of Leadership

To ensure fundraising remains a successful endeavor for your congregation/ organization, building up and maintaining confidence in leaders is key! The best place to start an effort for encouraging donors to give is demonstrating that the leadership of any particular institution can be trusted with all gifts that they will receive. To achieve this, there must be a long-term effort by all leaders, clergy or lay and volunteer or staff, to commit to transparency in financial matters by communicating and reporting clearly and *often* to congregants and constituents, and especially by putting policies and procedures in written form, and of course making them available as appropriate on websites or when requested by constituents.

Building trust and confidence in the leaders of a congregation or organization among its various donors and supporters will always be the starting point in my work with Episcopal parishes, dioceses, and other organizations. Without trust and confidence, supporters will not easily give current gifts nor be committed to make substantial gifts in the future through their estates. The challenge is made especially difficult when leaders frequently change at an organization.

To help build and maintain trust, there must be a "cultural commitment," regardless if individual leaders change. All leaders must commit to giving regular reports in written and public forums on the status of how gifts have been used, to avoiding deficit budgets (yes, a great challenge for many, and one which needs to be addressed in a separate volume), and to communicating the difference that your congregation/organization makes in the lives of its members/constituents, and especially how lives have been improved beyond the walls of your church or institution.

With respect to stewarding an organization's assets, leaders can inspire donors to give by demonstrating there has been a strategic and thoughtful process regarding SRI choices, as well as careful, ongoing monitoring of investment results with qualified professionals. Additionally, ensuring that leaders follow the wishes of donors regarding all gifts (endowment or otherwise designated) and that they never overspend or use funds for purposes the donors did not intend will also maintain trust and confidence. All of these efforts enhance the level of trust and confidence among constituents and clearly demonstrate that leaders are being good stewards of all of the funds they oversee. Your denomination or denominational foundation will likely also have resources to assist you with all of this important work and can help your leaders build up that sense of trust and confidence through a variety of ways.

I have been happy to witness more and more religious organizations, and many congregations too, finally focusing on raising more planned gifts from their members/constituents. Though some have been doing this work faithfully for decades, due to leadership changes and other issues, many congregations/organizations have neglected this crucial part of their stewardship ministry. Not only is encouraging planned giving a good thing for raising assets to fund your future ministries, those efforts also enable those supporters most committed to your congregation/organization's mission to *raise your church or religious organization to the level of family in their estate plans.* This allows your most dedicated donors to become a part of the *future* good work that your congregation/organization will do! Please don't deny those committed supporters that opportunity to be a part of your future ministry. Please raise awareness to all, regardless of their age or their perceived economic circumstances. The largest planned gifts do not normally come from the obviously wealthy, but often from the unexpected yet highly committed member or constituent who has given regularly over many years.

As you may have surmised, stimulating donors to make current gifts to endowments or creating one of the many types of planned gifts remains my greatest passion. Unfortunately, I cannot elaborate more on these topics here, but please reach out to your denomination's resources (listed in this book's appendix) and also review the recap of the different types of planned gifts provided as a "quick reference" in the appendix. Yet please note, the main way that nearly every charity builds significant endowments and other investable assets is through realized planned gifts from donor estates or retirement assets.

One idea previously noted is to consider setting aside assets with a particular socially responsible goal, such as holding stock directly if your congregation/organization invests only in pooled funds or similar vehicles. Other options for setting assets aside beyond your endowment, or what might compose a small portion of it, might be a revolving loan fund or a community investment opportunity fund where the focus is primarily on its social impact return, not the actual financial yield. Such activity could be funded by one or more committed donors. If promoting such activity is chosen within your congregation/organization, please make certain that you have a plan and a commitment for *reporting* to your constituents on your efforts. The venue for reporting should fit your culture, but consider public reporting at an annual parish meeting, a "ministry recap" opportunity during your main service, or some other appropriate occasion in front of a large audience of current (and future potential) supporters, or report online or in a well-read internal publication from your congregation/organization. Making people aware of what is being done is the first step in finding donors who may wish to sponsor that work.

Most of the institutions that invest funds in an ESG or SRI manner are typically doing so with long-term invested or endowment funds. As previously written, some will invest in these ways and some will not. However, if your congregation/organization is incrementally moving in that direction, accept the good you are doing without expecting perfection and tell people about it! I recommend that you publicize your chosen actions and your incremental progress. Whether your work takes the form of shareholder engagement, participating in forms of impact investing within your local community, or choosing to invest proactively with ESG factors or other ways, please publicize it. Use appropriate venues and opportunities for explaining to your congregants/constituents why you are taking those actions. This will keep donors engaged, and should lead to greater support from new constituents. Some will be inspired to get involved by actively participating with your efforts by offering their time and talents; others will be inspired to provide support by making a financial gift. Please remember, though, people will likely only give if you let them know that they can!

Conclusion

Whatever you do, be creative, be public, and focus on telling *how* you did what you did and how it made a *difference*, especially if the impact extended beyond your own local congregation/organization. Don't forget that if you only invest in pooled funds, you can also share with donors and constituents any positive impacts achieved from participating in those pooled vehicles. For example, if your pooled funds incorporate positive ESG activities, such as expanding board diversity, you are also a part of that work, and can talk about what has been done on your behalf. Even if you cannot vote proxies or file shareholder resolutions, when you invest in pooled funds that incorporate ESG, you are still supporting that good work which is being done.

Your choices matter! Your participation and incremental actions can bring about more *good* in the world: good that will make a difference toward actual "real-world" benefits and may inspire even more support from donors both new and old.

Remember this: "Whoever sows sparingly will also reap sparingly, and whoever sows generously will also reap generously" (2 Cor. 9:6, NIV).

Chapter 10

Taking Decisive Action, One Step at a Time*

James W. Murphy

And God is able to provide you with every blessing in abundance, so that by always having enough of everything, you may share abundantly in every good work. (2 Cor. 9:8)

Taking decisive action incrementally. This book was meant to be many things: a primer, a historical reference, and a way to inspire church leaders with basic information and "real-world" experiences. Primarily it was meant to be a toolkit for learning and considering how to proceed, helping you to decide what steps are next for your congregation/organization.

As previously promoted in chapter 9, take the lessons from this book to continue building trust and confidence among your donors and supporters, demonstrating that your leaders will be good stewards/caretakers of the gifts you have and will receive in the future. Start with putting in place your policies (see chapters 2 and 3). This is more than practical advice for increasing current and future giving; it is the moral and right thing to do as well. This will not only put you in good stead for planning and preparation for the monitoring of your investments, but will also provide clearer guidance to both your leaders (even if those leaders change) and potential donors for how to do this important work. Consider, for your own context, how best to talk about the work you and other leaders at your congregation/organization have or will do in this area. What will inspire your constituents? Perhaps, if the desire is strong toward SRI, you may have opportunities to encourage new gifts and even the creation of new endowment or special funds for this purpose.

---

* This material, including organizations and websites noted, is provided for informational purposes only and should not be viewed as an endorsement or as investment, tax, or other professional advice.

This book is filled with references, ideas, and examples of what others from many different denominations and contexts have done regarding the possibility of investing in this way. Bearing in mind that many aspects and ideas may not fit perfectly for repeating in your context, please reflect together with other leaders on what *might* be done. As indicated in the early chapters, consider what assets you have to invest and consider what would be best for your congregation/organization. Most congregations do not have considerable assets to invest, and numerous smaller religious organizations may have very limited endowment funds and few assets in reserve that are not already committed to the direct support of their ongoing mission. However, for some first steps, reflect together, first among your primary leaders and then more broadly among your congregants/constituents. Assess everyone's commitment and areas of interest, then discuss among a large group of leaders the best next steps for your congregation/organization.

If there is consensus among the congregation/organization to take initial action, select a small group of leaders with experience in investing as well as in the mission of the congregation/organization (you may already have this group if you have an endowment or invested funds), then begin your review of how you wish to move ahead (see chapter 4). Review the early chapters (1 through 3) of this book again to ensure that you have the necessary documents and procedures in place so as to plan and oversee your efforts, or at a minimum to know what you may *not* have. This will help you to know the strategic discussions that still need to take place, and what new documentation may need to be drafted.

Check with your denomination or denominational foundation or other resources. (See our appendix of resources by denomination; if you don't find appropriate resources, you can search on the internet or review resources of a denomination most similar to your own or of other entities that you know.) The internet may provide examples of what documentation and plans you might develop, but you can also reach out to other local congregations/organizations. Perhaps this would be a new ecumenical opportunity for collaboration and friendship! Strangely, many churches, within the same denomination in close proximity to each other, do not have any ongoing relationship; you could break the ice using SRI. Will collaboration with other churches or entities be a part of your activism?

In addition to the non- or multidenominational organizations listed in our appendix and throughout our chapters, don't forget that there are also many secular resources. SRI is a growing area of investment and many mainstream investment houses will have resources available to you in a variety of forms. As previously noted, many larger investment firms incorporate ESG aspects into their ongoing investment decisions.

Also recall that, since so many religious organizations and congregations do not have the means or the expertise to invest in individual stocks and bonds, pooled funds of many different kinds may fit you well. Many denominational foundations or denominational investment resources may have SRI or ESG factors built into their options, and their staffs would surely be more than happy to assist your efforts.

If you do have the capacity to invest in individual stocks, this means you will have the ability to put forward shareholder resolutions, if you meet some specific requirements (see chapter 4). The decision to invest in this way must be done with care, as investing in the direct ownership of stock carries with it more inherent risk than investing in pools, due to reduced diversification. Risk of poor performance from holding a small number of stocks and bonds is mitigated by pooled funds, as those vehicles hold many diverse securities, so the risk to your portfolio is reduced. However, for some congregations/organizations, even if the majority of their assets are invested in pooled funds for their inherent advantages, some may make the strategic decision to hold a small portion of assets separately for some specific efforts, such as shareholder engagement. In fact, as noted in chapter 9, that may be an inspiration for a donor to fund such efforts.

As has been previously mentioned, not all people will come to the same conclusions regarding what is right for your congregation/organization regarding SRI/ESG. You can review the case studies following these chapters to see examples of how different entities, even within the same denomination, made very different investment decisions for a variety of reasons. Our goal with this book has been to inform, inspire, and empower you, not dictate what must be done. It is up to you and your leadership to choose the best next steps for your congregation/organization. All contributors hope that you will consider powerful, yet possibly small, "next steps" that you could take. Please always remember that the "good" often grows best incrementally. Or as has been attributed to one of the great saints of the twentieth century, Teresa of Calcutta, "We ourselves feel that what we are doing is just a drop in the ocean. But the ocean would be less because of that missing drop."[1]

---

1. Mother Teresa, Brainy Quote, accessed June 7, 2019, *https://www.brainyquote.com/quotes/mother_teresa_121243*.

Finally, before choosing any investment options, please seek the help of professional investment advisors, including those through your denomination or denominational foundation. A consideration in moving forward, especially if your entity chose NOT to invest its limited funds in SRI, could be to encourage the members of your congregation or your constituents to consider the options reviewed in the next chapter on individual decisions or to use resources like community or denominational credit unions. These choices are clearly yours to make, based upon your circumstances and needs; I encourage you always to reflect on your values first, then on how to implement those values in "real-world" and impactful ways, especially when you wish to invest faithfully.

> Suppose one of you wants to build a tower. Won't you first sit down and estimate the cost to see if you have enough money to complete it? (Luke 14:28, NIV)

Chapter 11

Individual Investor Decisions and Considerations*

Kathryn McCloskey

Socially responsible investing (SRI) is not only a question for your congregation or religious organization. Individuals can also direct their financial resources in ways that are consistent with their beliefs and morals. We hope that the information in this book has helped to inform you and raise your awareness of the many diverse aspects of SRI and ESG. Although as an individual investor you may not have access to all of the options discussed in this book, you may be able to make choices that reflect your values. Please always remember the caution that "perfection may be the enemy of the good" for individuals as well, and you should consider starting incrementally and initially focusing on what makes the most sense for you and your family before making any investment decisions. We also recommend that you seek appropriate professional legal, tax, and financial advice before finalizing any investment or financial decisions.

There are constantly evolving options for the individual, or "retail," investor. A self-assessment period of considering one's reasons for SRI or ESG investing is important, because it will help direct you to the services and funds that are best aligned to your needs.

The Basics

All individuals need to consider their financial needs over varying time horizons. Short-term finances need to cover household necessaries and maintenance and are generally kept in banks for access. Longer-term finances need to provide a source of income in retirement. Just like in traditional investing,

---

* This material, including organizations and websites noted, is provided for informational purposes only and should not be viewed as an endorsement or as investment, tax, or other professional advice.

the primary rationale for SRI is future financial stability, and the correct vehicles are required for achieving that stability.

There are SRI or ESG options to consider for both short-term and long-term investments.

Short-Term Finances

Nearly every individual will need to work with an FDIC insured organization that provides the ability to write checks, receive income, transfer funds, hold cash for a rainy day while earning a fair interest rate, offer access to mortgages and loans, and all of the other services normally needed for everyday living. For most Americans, commercial banks provide those services. However, many people choose to use credit unions to provide most if not all of those same basic services, and can participate in those credit unions based on a number of factors such as union membership, employment affiliation, residency requirements, and other qualifications. Credit unions not only service typically underbanked communities, they also provide finance to small businesses, community-based organizations, and affordable housing that undergird development for low- and mid-income neighborhoods and rural areas (see chapter 8). Checking, savings, credit card options, and many other services are available to members, and those who use them actively choose these credit unions to support their missions and additional socially focused or religious goals. In fact, many credit unions also may have a religious affiliation or origin, as evidenced by the many Roman Catholic credit unions throughout the country. Opening accounts in a credit union demonstrates an individual's commitment to their missions; often they frequently serve low- and mid-income communities and seek to improve the lives of those communities.

For example, there are options for some Episcopalians to invest in credit unions that serve various members of their dioceses. The Episcopal Community Federal Credit Union, based in the Episcopal diocese of Los Angeles, boasts that 40 percent of its membership are Hispanic, 30 percent African American, 20 percent Caucasian, and 10 percent other ethnicities.[1] Doing personal banking business with a credit union satisfies the goal of many committed Christians who wish their individual financial transactions to make a difference as well as a statement of their faith in action.

---

1. "Who We Are," Episcopal Federal Credit Union, accessed April 30, 2019, *https://efcula.org/about-us/*.

For some, credit unions may not be the only choice individuals make to show their faith in action. There are several ways to place small amounts of money aside for particular outcomes. Known also as impact investing, individuals are able to invest in retail notes to drive positive social or environmental outcomes. Individuals can make directed investments in women and small businesses, and clean energy community solutions can be made through a variety of organizations.

Impact investing platforms for individuals are beginning to offer outcome-specific ways to invest as well. With options like clean water, zero waste, and disease eradication, investors can use their expendable income to support progress.

Additionally, for many people, the most practical way to seek to make their everyday actions demonstrate their faith may be through other means, such as working with local organizations to improve the environment through recycling programs or supporting a variety of charities through their current giving. Speaking for all of the contributing authors of this book, we hope that you will include generous donations to your own faith community in which we hope you also participate actively, sharing your time, talents, prayers, and worship.

Long-Term Investments

There are many investment options for retail investors interested in pursuing sustainable investing, including mutual funds and exchange traded funds (ETFs), direct ownership of stocks, and community banking or fixed rate investing.

Pooled Investment Funds

Most individuals invest for the long term in pooled funds like mutual funds or ETFs. A mutual fund is a cost-effective way for people to invest alongside other individuals. Exchange-traded funds are similar to mutual funds, but they typically track the index to which they are benchmarked, i.e., the Standard & Poor's 500, and don't try to deviate for stock picking or quantitative reasons that mutual funds sometimes employ. Neither mutual funds nor ETFs may be directed to invest or not invest in certain things by the ultimate investor, the individual. As such, it is most appropriate for an individual interested in investing sustainably to do their research before investing; after investing it will be impossible to sway the practices of that fund. Moving investments will be the only viable option at that point.

Unless otherwise stated, it is likely that the pooled funds available from the largest investment managers are not using SRI precepts to guide the decision-making process. However, a fund's documentation, or prospectus, will outline what its ethical or ESG processes are. As previously written about, there continues to be a growing focus and demand for these types of investments, so even more options would be expected to be available to individual investors in the future.

One resource to determine the sustainability of a pooled fund can be found at Morningstar, an investment research platform. Morningstar Sustainability Ratings sets a sustainability score for many of the most popular mutual funds and ETFs. The sustainability rating can be located when looking at a fund's description. Registration to Morningstar is required to view the rating. This registration is free at the time of writing.[2]

Most mainline Protestant denominations have a pension scheme for their affiliated workers—clergy, lay workers of health and human service organizations, etc. These pension plans frequently use SRI concepts—informed by faith, though they may deviate for various reasons from denominational guidelines—as the basis for their plans. There are not as many faith-based investment pooled funds available to lay individuals as are available to churches and institutions; however, it's important to know that there are some.

Many individuals are concerned with whether their investments are too involved in the fossil fuel industries. There are websites that allow individuals to learn more about their mutual funds' fossil fuel exposures.

Owning Stocks

Many individuals, through electronic trading accounts and otherwise, directly own shares in companies. There are ways to express environmental and social viewpoints as a shareholder, or partial owner, of a corporation. The most straightforward way to express an ESG view is to vote accordingly during the company's annual meeting. Many like-minded institutions file shareholder resolutions seeking better governance or operational control over environmental impacts or social and workforce impacts. In this way, voting for shareholder resolutions is an imperative feedback mechanism

---

2. Morningstar, accessed April 30, 2019, *https://www.morningstar.com.*

for the companies in which individuals are invested. The virtuous cycle of shareholder feedback encourages publicly traded companies to publish corporate responsibility or sustainability reports, which outline ESG policies and performance.

As a partial owner in a corporation, an individual investor with shares may have the right to file shareholder resolutions on topics of environmental or social improvements that one believes a company should make. The process of filing shareholder resolutions is challenging because of the rules outlined by the Securities and Exchange Commission (SEC), but it is possible.

United Church Funds has worked with a motivated individual investor in the past who used his shares in a company to call for change. This person was a scientist who became alarmed with the implications of climate change and global warming and began to make changes in his life. Not only did he invest in solar panels and buy a hybrid vehicle, he began lobbying for policy and legislation to curb carbon pollution. This person bought shares in a utility that generates 80 percent of their electricity from coal, which is twice the national average. He began working with a group of socially responsible institutional investors on efforts regarding water and coal ash issues with that company, and then submitted a shareholder resolution with the company to report more fully on their lobbying and whether it was antithetical to improving environmental outcomes. He invited other United Church of Christ investing bodies, including United Church Funds, to support his resolution by cofiling. United Church Funds did so. The resolution ultimately received 41 percent support by all outstanding shares of that company. This is a very high vote, and made the company make considerable concessions.

Planned Giving

When considering how to effectively give to your congregation or any religious charity you support, there are options for individuals to leave a legacy knowing that their gift is being administered in a socially responsible way. Trusting that the congregation or religious organization has put in place endowment and gift acceptance policies and built trust among its constituent donors, most individuals can make a gift to the institutions they have loved and supported during their lifetimes through their will, trust, or other designations upon death from various accounts. In addition to standard bequests and similar allocations, there are numerous ways to leave a planned gift such as through insurance, life estate in real estate, and many other ways, and especially through leaving the remainder value of tax deferred accounts like IRAs, 401(k), or 403(b) options.

Many religious institutions administer planned giving programs to enable donors to make significant gifts out of their estate or other assets they hold for retirement. Nearly all of the denominational foundations listed in this book's appendix offer resources and guidance for how to encourage these special types of gifts. In fact, most of those organizations also offer to interested donors the more complex life income gifts, such as charitable gift annuities (CGA), pooled income funds (PIF), and various kinds of charitable remainder trusts (CRUT/CRAT), which can provide individuals income for life in exchange for a charitable gift, with the remainder being given to the congregation or designated entity at the income beneficiary's death.

One of the most flexible and fastest-growing giving options is the donor-advised fund, or DAF. DAFs are giving vehicles one can establish to provide a current tax deduction and then enable opportunities to recommend future grants to benefit a great number of charities. In addition to the many sponsoring charities created by large institutional investors that provide DAFs, many of your denominational foundations have also created DAFs to serve their donors. DAFs are usually easy to set up and allow donors to make a charitable contribution of cash, appreciated assets, or other assets, receive an immediate tax deduction for the entire gift, and then make future grants to one or more charities (often within their denomination) from the fund over time. When combined with socially responsible investing choices, an individual using these philanthropic tools is empowering the full life cycle of giving.

We wish you well as you consider all of these many options for yourself and your family. Before you finalize any investments or gifts, please consult with an appropriate professional legal, tax, or other professional advisor to ensure not only that you are acting in your and your family's best interest but also that all of your wishes, including those for responsible investing, will be fulfilled.

Introduction to Case Studies

James W. Murphy

First and foremost, the following case studies are not meant to provide a *perfect* or comprehensive review of SRI or ESG. All entities in our case studies have chosen to take decisive and incremental actions to implement their efforts; these case studies are meant to give our readers hope and inspiration for what may be possible for them, both now and in the future. The goal of these case studies is to bring together many of the principles reviewed in our chapters and to demonstrate that though numerous congregations and religious organizations initially struggled with SRI and ESG, all benefited from the process. These real-life stories, with some of the interviewees remaining confidential, were just that—*real life*—and are meant to motivate you with their honesty!

For these entities, many public and confidential meetings took place and much collaboration was sought, in addition to a great amount of time spent reflecting upon and reviewing the financial implications of their decisions. Some congregations and organizations will take months to analyze their options; I hope you will choose to start out slowly in appropriate and practical ways that fit your context. However, not every congregation or organization will choose in the end to invest using SRI or ESG principles, for a variety of reasons.

We have sought to have a wide variety of denominations and contexts in these examples so that readers may be able to see their own congregation or organization in these case studies. For example, most Roman Catholic parishes and some other entities may not be able to hold assets directly and must rely on other entities or higher judicatories to do that on their behalf. Some denominations have robust foundations that ably serve the denomination throughout the entire country, with multiple options for investment by congregations and other entities; some require that assets be managed more locally or in a strict manner without any local variation. And, as will be demonstrated soon, investment committees at different organizations within the same denomination may choose to invest very differently. There is not one singular path, and that is actually a good thing.

After completing all of these chapters and case studies, please do review our appendix for further assistance as you continue on your journey to invest faithfully, but also please choose well, cautiously, and collaboratively.

Blessings on your journey!

Lessons of Collaboration on Socially Responsible Investing*

James W. Murphy

Many entities have made the choice to move forward with implementing SRI with their assets, whether they are congregations, religious organizations, religious communities of sisters, or overseeing judicatories. In the following article, I reached out to four different entities to get their perspectives on the challenges they faced, the choices they made, and the processes they went through to get there. What was similar among all those interviewed? A desire to live out their faith through the investment choices they made. What was different were the processes and journeys for getting there. Some sought to implement SRI for their local congregation and then chose to move beyond; some always wanted to choose SRI and never questioned their plan; and others had concerns that continue to this day regarding their fiduciary duties. A key learning among all was that collaboration, and often compromise and incremental change, was key to implementing their goals, both at the local and national level.

Speaking with a Unitarian Universalist Association (UUA)–related entity, I discovered a great conviction to do good in the world and to invest faithfully. However, this entity also wanted to ensure that they were good stewards and good fiduciaries of the assets they oversaw. As congregations and other entities in the UUA are never forced to conform, but simply encouraged to follow the actions at their national gathering, called the General Assembly, there is always much discussion in Unitarian circles on actions to be taken. In this case the entity's leaders discussed the issues surrounding the divestment of fossil fuels and whether or not it was better to remain invested so that a *seat at the table* could be retained. Additionally, the leaders

---

* This material, including organizations and websites noted, is provided for informational purposes only and should not be viewed as an endorsement or as investment, tax, or other professional advice.

of this entity debated if a middle ground could be found regarding fossil fuel divestment. Their discussions were not completed quickly, but extended over several years. Fiduciary concerns were raised, such as whether their investments were diversely invested enough to provide the best long-term possibility for asset growth, as well as if positive investing factors, beyond a singular focus on excluding fossil fuel investments, could continue to be considered.

Over time and after numerous leadership discussions, this entity chose to take several steps forward. They set themselves on a path of gradual reduction in fossil fuel holdings. Using ESG ratings as an important part of their investment strategy, some leaders promoted that their entity should provide some of their capital to enhance community loans and development in a variety of under-resourced areas. Similarly, our readers may find that their own discussions may inspire and change minds through open and ongoing conversations, which allow for leaders to change and adapt incrementally.

On a somewhat different path, I spoke with a UUA congregation that chose to be a leader in their local region and then pursued having an impact on a resolution for fossil fuel divestment for their entire denomination. Inspired after listening to several UUA leaders promoting divestment in fossil fuels and advocating for economic transformation to a sustainable energy economy, leaders at this congregation encouraged first their own congregation to divest, and then began to collaborate with other local leaders to lead an initiative to pass resolutions to promote divestment and reinvestment in alternative energy within their geographic region. In time these leaders realized that to have a broader impact they would need to expand their efforts and offer resolutions at their UUA General Assembly regarding these topics.

According to the leader I spoke with, eventually many of the UUA leaders involved in these efforts came to the realization that to get some of the goals accomplished within the legislative process of their very diverse-thinking denomination, they would need to collaborate and compromise. There were also the challenges for other leaders who believed that their fiduciary duties may not allow them to divest or to take on much greater risk with new "alternative" energy investments, which did not have a long history of performance. Instead of passing a resolution calling for a complete and near-immediate divestment, a compromise resolution was put forward and approved to allow some fossil fuel assets still to be held by the national UUA organization so that further shareholder engagement could take place. As reported to me, for those fully committed to complete divestment this felt like a defeat, as they believed that fossil fuel companies were not worth the burdensome work of engagement.

However, by accepting that compromise, a resolution passed not calling for complete divestment all at once, but allowing for a more gradual change.[1]

Similarly, speaking with a representative of a United Church of Christ (UCC) congregation, their leaders also demonstrated the importance of diligence when pursuing SRI and the importance of interacting and collaborating over time with denominational leadership. The leaders of this congregation through various adult learning opportunities had made the discussions surrounding SRI, and specifically fossil fuel divestment, a key topic. In addition to numerous actions actively supported by members of the congregation to encourage better water and waste disposal practices, installing solar panels, and various other opportunities for activism for social justice causes, there was also a great desire to divest from fossil fuels.

Since the parish did not have a large endowment, there were several discussions on whether or not the congregation should even pursue divestment, and there was no immediate willingness to invest in a new fossil-free fund being created by the UCC's foundation, United Church Funds (UCF). (In fact, the new fund required $10 million of initial capital from multiple UCC investors to be set up.) However, the congregation through its well-attended and reliable adult education efforts openly discussed the issues. Leaders at this congregation came to a consensus that even with the risk of investing in a new fund and the fear of underperformance due to reduced diversification, the congregation would move forward with this investment at UCF.

Though this congregation was early in their commitment to this new fund, others took more time to confirm their willingness to participate in it. Thankfully, enough UCC entities eventually committed a sufficient amount of assets for the fund to be created, but it took many months. This is another example of the importance of collaboration and commitment to a goal, but also a recognition that all of our organizations invest and exist in the "real world," where there are threshold amounts to create funds that match SRI goals. Perfection can rarely be achieved, but through collaboration and compromise very good things can be accomplished.

Finally, a very different example comes from a former chair of the board of directors of a foundation benefiting a United Methodist church. The foundation had articles of incorporation and bylaws, as with any incorporated 501(c)(3). It also had a well-developed investment policy statement that included all the usual elements: investment objectives, personnel designations, prohibited

---

1. "Fossil Fuel Divestment: 2014 Business Resolution," Unitarian Universalist Association, accessed June 1, 2019, *https://www.uua.org/action/statements/fossil-fuel-divestment*.

and allowable instruments and investments, asset allocation ranges, and social principles to guide investment decisions and to seek better behaviors by and within the companies owned that would bolster investment performance. In exploring the latter element, the board was guided by the denomination's Book of Discipline provisions relating to socially responsible investment, as well as by various resolutions that have been adopted through the years relating to socially responsible investment. They were fully on board with investing in an SRI manner from the beginning, and considering non-SRI options never even came up as something to discuss! This may not be the experience of your congregation/ organization, but uniform agreement can occur, even on SRI.

For your further insight, I share the following details for this same church regarding their particular internal practices and also reference the documents which they used. The *2016 United Methodist Book of Discipline*, par. 717, provides, "All United Methodist [local churches and foundations] shall endeavor to seek investments in institutions, companies, corporations, or funds that promote racial and gender justice, protect human rights, prevent the use of sweatshop or forced labor, avoid human suffering, and preserve the natural world, including mitigating the effects of climate change." It further provides, "In addition, United Methodist [local churches and foundations] shall endeavor to avoid investments in companies engaged in core business activities that are not aligned with the Social Principles through their direct or indirect involvement with the production of anti-personnel weapons and armaments (both nuclear and conventional weapons), alcoholic beverages or tobacco; or that are involved in privately operated correctional facilities, gambling, pornography or other forms of exploitative adult entertainment."[2] While the UMC Book of Discipline provisions should be viewed as a minimum or starting point in socially responsible investment, they were not the only resource used by their foundation. The United Methodist Church also maintains a Book of Resolutions containing resolutions approved by the denomination's General Conference covering a host of social issues.

The board of directors of this congregation's foundation annually reviews its investment and spending policy for social responsibility and other provisions such as asset allocation and personnel. Most recently, the board added the prohibition above for private prison management companies. With some of their assets in direct stock holdings, at least once each year their board

---

2. The Book of Discipline, ¶ 717, "Sustainable and Socially Responsible Investments," the United Methodist Church, accessed July 28, 2019, *http://www.umc.org/what-we-believe/para-717-socially-responsible-investments*.

meets with its equity managers to review holdings, with a special eye toward their social commitments, including a review of updated lists of prohibited companies derived from the screening of the broad social investment prohibitions. As a quantitative matter, the list contains companies that derive no greater than a very small percentage of profits from the prohibited activity (e.g., 5 to 10 percent). No company can be entirely guaranteed to derive zero profit, directly or indirectly, from a prohibited activity at any one point in time. This is another example of choosing to do good without trying to impose a standard of perfection that might make investing very difficult to impossible (see chapter 3)!

Their board also was able to review proxy voting policies by equity managers through their regional Methodist foundation. The 2016 United Methodist Book of Discipline requires that local churches and foundations consider investment of funds through the United Methodist area (regional) foundation serving their judicatory. Unlike many other denominations, which rely primarily on their denomination or denominational foundation for investing endowments throughout the country, local regionalized Methodist foundations serve churches within their own geographic region. In their case, which is also quite rare, stock shares were held in the name of their church's foundation and not in pooled funds. As such, the congregation's foundation was poised to take the next step to develop a list of shareholder advocacy priorities and to seek the partnership of their local area coalition for socially responsible investment to file resolutions with a few companies owned.

Something this congregation's foundation does, which many other religious organizations could consider, is that while the seven members of the board of this foundation are largely chosen for investment experience and expertise, other members with a passion for social advocacy are also included. To encourage stronger education of the congregation and furthering socially responsible investment in turn by church members, foundation bylaws include typical provisions for classes of directors with term limits and rotation on an annual basis; the senior pastor of the congregation is ensured a seat on the board as well. The social policies of the United Methodist Church and the actions taken in the past by this local congregation helped to demystify the steps involved in this powerful area of ministry.

What might your congregation/organization do in similar circumstances? Clearly seeking consensus and maintaining collaboration is key to future successes. How else can your leaders, lay and clergy, reflect together on your "best next steps"?

Same Denomination, Very Different Choices*

James W. Murphy

A central theme of this book is that we are not seeking to prescribe an exact way of doing SRI and want to demonstrate that different entities will make very different choices when it comes to investing in various ways. After reading this book and following significant reflection, some congregations/ organizations may make the informed decision that they do not wish to invest in that manner; or they may wish to focus on certain aspects like fossil fuel divestment; or they may simply choose to invest in secular funds, or with their denominational foundation, which has set up pooled investment options to serve their denominational needs. And some may choose to use a small portion of their invested funds to buy specific stocks so that they may engage in shareholder advocacy. As a part of seeking to demonstrate that con-gregations and institutions will come to very different conclusions and final actions, I share the experiences of three Episcopal Church Foundation (ECF)[1] clients below. So as not to reveal our clients and their individual choices, we will treat these three clients anonymously as we recount their decisions.

Reflecting that truly Anglican (Episcopalians are a part of the world-wide Anglican Communion led by the archbishop of Canterbury as "first among equals") perspective found in our traditional attitude toward the act of confession—*all may, none must, some should*—I thought it would

---

* This material, including organizations and websites noted, is provided for informational purposes only and should not be viewed as an endorsement or as investment, tax, or other professional advice.

1. The Episcopal Church Foundation is an independent, lay-led organization that serves the entire Episcopal denomination in various programs and services focused on leadership and financial resource development. ECF supports the planned giving and investment management needs of the Episcopal Church's parishes, dioceses, and various organizations. ECF's endowment program is very flexible and allows for access to types of socially responsible investing, if desired, for clients currently investing over $100K.

be helpful for our readers to reflect on three actual ECF clients who made very different SRI decisions. Congregations and organizations from different denominations often come to very different SRI choices, but even entities within the *same* denomination may have very different strategies for how to invest faithfully.

The first entity I interviewed had previously invested using existing SRI options (which excluded investments in gambling, tobacco, and weapons manufacturing, for example) provided by ECF, but eventually chose to stop imposing any exclusions that had been a part of the standard screen. Their leadership had significant concerns that the screening may be limiting their performance from less diversification. In their case, they felt that even small amounts of underperformance could have a significant impact on their ability to meet current ministry needs. In their view, their fiduciary duty to maximize return outweighed the desire of some to exclude certain industries from their portfolio. Their leadership also felt that by maximizing their return, any additional appreciation would help them to support their other ministries. Given a wide variety of opinions among the leadership, many felt there were so many potential exclusions that might be considered, both now and in the future, that for stability and the capability to ensure a diverse investment mix, they did not want to be held back at all. Leaders also felt that "emotional reactions" entered into every discussion on SRI, especially those surrounding the defense industry and fossil fuel divestment. For these leaders, the reason to invest or not invest seemed to be less "rational" and outside of their main fiduciary duties to ensure the best return possible. Given that they did not have an extremely large endowment to begin with, leaders believed they needed to remain "data driven" primarily on performance as opposed to investing to "feel better about themselves."

When asked if this entity continues to be satisfied with their decision, they affirmed that they were. However, those leaders who had previously been supportive of exclusions were also satisfied that ECF's investment vendor always kept ESG factors and adherence to UNPRI guidelines as a part of their investing decisions, though not the only factors for whether or not to invest in particular companies (see chapter 3). Some of those ESG aspects that the vendor takes under consideration include such issues as board diversity and adding more women to corporate boards, efficient and proactive usage of water and other resources, as well as proactive hiring of a diverse workforce. Maintaining ESG factors as a part of the investment decision remained important to these particular leaders, but they also desired that monitoring other future macro trends and evaluating ongoing performance would be considered more seriously, including enhancing investment diversification.

Another Episcopal entity, up to the writing of this case study, continues to use an SRI option, which exclude some sin stocks: gambling, tobacco, weapons manufacturing, etc. Though some of their leaders are satisfied that they use these SRI exclusions, many of their leaders are indifferent as to whether they are being used or not, and favor focusing on ensuring the highest return on their investments. Like the first entity, they are very concerned about performance and diversification, and though satisfied with keeping SRI exclusions in place, they would be willing to make a change and remove the screens if performance were ever to decline significantly. To date, as performance has been more than acceptable, a change from SRI has not been raised. However, this entity wishes to remain on a *via media* on the topic, as they feel that their main fiduciary duty is to maximize returns so that they can do the most good to improve people's lives through the many ministries that their endowment supports. In fact, the investment committee of this entity actively chose not to move assets into carbon-free investing options, to ensure maintaining appropriate diversification of their portfolio, when this issue was being actively discussed at the wider church level.

Not having a very large endowment either, this entity believes that their work in ministry and advocacy of people is central to their mission, but they do not feel that their endowment should be used as a central tool in that effort. They are much more in favor of maximizing return to ensure that their ministries are funded, which they believe brings about much good in their local context and the wider world. However, many of their leaders are also encouraged by the proactive investing and the use of ESG factors to ensure long-term performance and returns.

Our third ECF client example is an entity that has taken a very different perspective from the other two, and has actively chosen to invest in funds that exclude fossil fuel companies. Many of its leaders desired to support the growing movement throughout the Episcopal Church to divest of fossil fuel assets. Although they too had many concerns about the long-term growth impact that divestment may have on their endowment, and expressed a concern about maintaining enough diversification, they felt that divestment was still important enough to pursue, and in fact that it may be financially *prudent* to get out of fossil fuel investments. Many people believe that it is financially imprudent to stay invested in fossil fuel companies, especially those with significant assets in oil, gas, or coal reserves, due to the possible future imposition of "carbon taxes" or similar efforts. Many feel that there is significant risk in the devaluation of these assets if they ever become "stranded" due to government action or the implementation of new technologies that would not rely on fossil fuels.

This client remains very happy with their decision as well. Their leaders and constituents remain committed to divestment of fossil fuels and performance of their investments to date has been good. Though their endowment is also not substantial, they hope that their choices will inspire donors to give additional gifts to their endowment (see chapter 9). However, their leaders are also monitoring performance carefully and are willing to discuss the possibility of changing their plans if performance would suffer over the long term.

I highlight these examples not to discourage your congregation from considering SRI or divestment, but in an effort to highlight that these are decisions your leaders should consider carefully. Many leaders believe it is their obligation to encourage the maximum return on their investments, so as to provide a reliable income stream to support existing ministries. Balancing return with various other important goals needs to be in the forefront of church leaders' minds. Leaders should always take into account the risk of excluding offending industries—which may reduce diversification—and the potential, though not certainty, of lower returns. However, is a more proactive ESG approach in investing more appropriate for your congregation/ organization? All of these issues require time, reflection, and ongoing discussion, and there are many issues for your leadership to consider before finalizing your plans.

Values Meet Reality: A Roman Catholic Institutional Approach*

*Bobbi Hannigan***

Catholic Extension, located in Chicago, Illinois, was founded in 1905 to raise funds to help build churches and the Church itself in poor communities across the United States. Today, Catholic Extension continues that mission through capacity-building grants and strategic initiatives. One of these strategic initiatives is a pooled investment fund to help smaller dioceses and parishes combine their assets to access world-class investing strategies to achieve their long-term investment return goals. Through this fund, Catholic Extension has taken on the fiduciary responsibility of investing over $150 million in assets to serve over fifty bishops and their dioceses. Implementing an investment strategy that incorporates Catholic socially responsible investing (SRI) for the diverse group of investors has been an exciting and rewarding endeavor. However, it also exposed the realities of the lack of options available to effectively invest according to Catholic social teaching. Catholic Extension developed a workable solution to fulfill its fiduciary obligation that dovetailed very nicely with the SRI guidelines from the United States Conference of Catholic Bishops (USCCB).

The USCCB SRI guidelines can be summarized in two key principles:

1. Exercise responsible financial stewardship.
2. Exercise ethical and social stewardship in an investment policy.

The application of these interdependent principles should result in competitive investment returns that (1) avoid participation in harmful activities

---

* This material, including organizations and websites noted, is provided for informational purposes only and should not be viewed as an endorsement or as investment, tax, or other professional advice.

** Editor's note: Catholic Extension is an organization that has been doing good work for the Roman Catholic Church in the United States for nearly 115 years. This case study is an example of how SRI standards were implemented in an effective way, both strategically and incrementally, over a period of time.

(avoid evil); (2) leverage the role as stockholder to support policies in accord with Catholic values and oppose those in conflict with them; and (3) promote the common good. A key expectation of the guidelines is to ensure that an investment policy addresses the following areas: protecting human life, promoting human dignity, reducing arms production, pursuing economic justice, protecting the environment, and encouraging corporate responsibility.[1]

It is no small task to responsibly execute the expectations underlying the USCCB's SRI guidelines. The USCCB recognized this challenge and expected investors to act with common sense and in good faith, noting that there may be limited resources and staff to achieve perfection. Even so, the guidelines counseled that any lapse in oversight could result in the appearance of scandal of benefitting from activities that contradict Catholic social teaching. This case study recounts one of the ways taken to meet this challenge.

From the start of building the pooled fund, Catholic Extension, with help from its investment consultant, first developed an investment policy that included the following components:

- An "endowment model" approach that has diversification among a variety of asset classes that are not correlated with each other;
- A bias toward passive strategies in highly researched, efficient markets, supplemented by active strategies, especially in the less efficient markets (e.g., emerging markets, small-cap equities);
- A tilt toward value managers, as these have proven to outperform growth managers over the long term; and
- A standard deviation of performance (i.e., volatility or risk exposure) that represents a fair tradeoff against long-term returns.

This approach is typical for any long-term investor, especially an institution that has a fiduciary responsibility for generating competitive returns necessary for funding the mission.

Next, Catholic Extension established the process for applying the USCCB SRI guidelines within the context of the investment policy. The first step for any asset class is to identify best-in-class managers, preferably those whose performance is in the top quartile. The second step is to evaluate a

---

1. The full description of the USCCB SRI guidelines is available at *http://www.usccb.org/about/financial-reporting/socially-responsible-investment-guidelines.cfm.*

manager's compliance with USCCB SRI guidelines. This is accomplished with the use of a third-party screening service that identifies companies not complying with the USCCB SRI criteria and compares the list to a potential manager's historical Security Exchange Commission 13F filings that list their underlying holdings. Assuming a manager's performance and SRI compliance are acceptable, and an investment is made, the manager is informed of our SRI requirements and our proxy voting preferences. The third step is ongoing oversight of compliance by reviewing their quarterly 13F filings. The fourth step is in keeping with the USCCB guidelines to influence the marketplace by contacting any manager whose holdings include restricted companies and asking them to liquidate. In some cases, that starts an ongoing correspondence in which the hope is that this will influence their investment decisions in the future. When a manager's investments are consistently following a strategy in conflict with Catholic social teaching, the fifth step is to liquidate the investment and start the process over again to find a new manager.

While the process sounds rather straightforward, the reality is that this is much harder to implement consistently. We found the universe of desired managers did not have off-the-shelf USCCB SRI-compliant funds. However, after much research, Catholic Extension came to the realization that many fund managers, whether they knew it or not, were *not* investing in conflict with Catholic social teaching. We also discovered that various studies have estimated that up to 10 percent of the global equity market would be out of compliance with the USCCB SRI guidelines. This implies that, all else being equal, 90 percent of fund managers' investment decisions therefore could be compliant and expanded the potential universe beyond SRI-branded funds. So the decision was made to invest in managers that have been historically in compliance with USCCB SRI, knowing full well they could fall out of compliance in the future. The overriding theme became "trust but verify." That approach has worked rather well over the last six years, with only a few managers being terminated, including an international fund that had very strong performance relative to its benchmark, a perfect example of where values met reality. To avoid manager turnover like this, a separately managed account arrangement, if available, can be a viable solution, but only if it is cost effective.

Finding appropriate fund managers continues to be a challenge, although it is getting better. Early on we achieved some easy wins, such as identifying index funds for large-cap US and developed markets that had a USCCB SRI screen. Wading into the emerging universe of USCCB SRI-branded funds found that, unfortunately, many funds either did not have the investment strategies we desired (e.g., value tilt), were not close to top-quartile performance, had unacceptably high fees for the returns generated, or, most disturbingly, actually invested in noncompliant companies! These issues were more common five or six years ago, and with the trends in ESG investing there has been a steady growth in fund managers willing to provide a USCCB SRI option. Where we once could only find managers with a USCCB SRI compliant strategy to cover just 15 percent of our investments in 2012, we have progressively increased coverage to over 50 percent.

Even with the steady growth of fund managers offering USCCB SRI-branded funds, it is still a very fragmented market and offerings in areas such as emerging markets are hard to find. Given the lack of a proven track record, it is no surprise that the USCCB does not endorse any financial advisors or investment firms offering SRI-branded funds. So the current "trust but verify" process described above will continue to guide our decisions until the market matures. While 99.9 percent of the fund's assets are currently compliant, we remain vigilant.

It has been our experience that applying a practical and consistent process to a well-diversified investment portfolio can successfully address the fiduciary obligations and the USCCB SRI guidelines without sacrificing market returns. In these current times, when the Catholic Church needs to practice transparently what it teaches, our bishops especially appreciate this service and support our continued commitment to influence managers to consider Catholic social teaching in their investment decisions.

Denominational SRI Issues*

Joseph M. Kinard and James W. Murphy

Each denomination seeks to do good and hopes to advance the gospel through its many internal processes, even if to onlookers (and even to many on the inside) it appears to be a seemingly endless series of committee meetings, overly detailed discussions, compromise deals, and multiple votes. Even within more hierarchical churches, where there is much less congregational participation in denominational decisions, processes for changing liturgies or the adoption of something like socially responsible investing (SRI) can take great amounts of time for discussion and review, and requires collaboration among many constituencies.

As previously elaborated, the choice of exactly what to do about SRI in your congregation/organization will vary. Some constituents will lobby for excluding specific industries from portfolios, and others will support buying individual securities so that the denomination will have a voice at the board table. Those responsible for these decisions must consider their fiduciary duties for overseeing the assets entrusted to them and decide the best ways to invest faithfully while ensuring that they meet the obligations for their ministries, from keeping the lights on and the air conditioning running, to ensuring that staff members receive their weekly pay. These discussions will happen in individual congregations as well as religious charities like denominational social service agencies, but when these considerations are being reviewed at most national denominational gatherings and various denominational committee meetings, the amount of conversation, disagreement, and need for collaboration increases exponentially. This case study reviews how several very different denominations have handled various SRI issues in recent years.

---

* This material, including organizations and websites noted, is provided for informational purposes only and should not be viewed as an endorsement or as investment, tax, or other professional advice.

In this case study we begin with an extensive review of how the Presbyterian Church (USA) dealt with several aspects of SRI over time, as well as with respect to proposals for divestment and boycotts regarding the Middle East. We follow that with interviews with denominational leaders from the Episcopal Church, United Church of Christ (UCC), and the Disciples of Christ. Each of these traditions has their own national gatherings and processes, and instead of going deeply into each of them, we will focus on some of the important aspects of what each has been able to accomplish.

A Presbyterian Process: A Deep Dive

The Presbyterian Church (USA) has a long history of utilizing church investments for mission purposes, beginning with the Confession of 1967, a foundational document for investment policies based on reconciliation and the belief that Jesus Christ directs all aspects of our lives, including stewardship of money.[1] Fast-forward to 1971 and the belief that investment is "an instrument of mission and includes theological, social and economic considerations."[2] In 1971, the Presbyterian Church (USA) became a founding member of the Interfaith Center on Corporate Responsibility (ICCR) in recognition of the church's unique opportunity to advance its mission faithfully through financial resources entrusted to it. The issue at that time which most motivated the Presbyterian Church (USA) was apartheid in South Africa. During that process, a committee on socially responsible investment was created: Mission Responsibility Through Investment (MRTI). MRTI was set up to implement General Assembly policies on socially responsible investing by engaging corporations in which the church owns stock directly: using dialogues, voting shareholder proxies, filing shareholder resolutions, correspondence, and recommending actions to others in the church.

The Committee on MRTI has twelve members, including trustees of the Board of Pensions, Presbyterian Foundation, Presbyterian Mission Agency Board, Advisory Committee on Women's Concerns, Racial Equity Advocacy Committee, Advisory Committee on Social Witness Policy, and three at-large members elected by the General Assembly. MRTI is lodged in the Compassion, Peace, and Justice Ministry Program, whose mission goals

---

1. "Inclusive Language Version of the Confession of 1967," Presbyterian Church (USA) Presbyterian Mission, March 17, 2010, *https://www.presbyterianmission.org/resource/inclusive-language-version-confession-1967/*.

2. *Corporate Social Responsibility Investment Policy Guidelines*, adopted by the 183rd General Assembly of the United Presbyterian Church (USA) in 1971, *https://www.presbyterianmission.org/wp-content/uploads/mrti_ga_policy_-_1971l.pdf*.

are the pursuit of peace; racial, social, economic, and women's justice; and environmental responsibility.

Presbyterians do not make rash decisions; there is a fundamental belief expressed as doing things in a good and decent order. Congregations are locally governed by lay and teaching elders in groups called sessions. Representatives from sessions are sent to regional bodies named presbyteries. Presbyteries utilize overtures, or preliminary resolutions, to delineate and promulgate issues of political, social, and international concern. Presbyteries then elect commissioners to attend the General Assembly every two years. For overtures to advance to General Assembly, they require "concurrence" from other presbyteries.

As mentioned, the church believes money and investments have a significant place in our society. While corporations can provide positive work environments, help create sustainable communities, and operate in harmony with creation, they can also damage the natural world, pay less than living wages, and produce harmful products. When that happens, the church must respond in a thoughtful, deliberate manner. Hence the requirement for a conflict resolution process that could ultimately lead to divestment from a corporation if engagement fails. To that end, seven criteria for divestment were developed by the MRTI Committee.

1. The issue on which divestment is proposed should be one reflecting central aspects of the faith.
2. The issue on which divestment is proposed should be one that the church has addressed by a variety of educational and action efforts, such as (a) correspondence with companies; (b) discussions with company managers and directors; (c) statements, questions, and shareholder resolutions at stockholder meetings; and (d) legal action against corporations.
3. The analysis supporting the proposed (a) should be clearly grounded in the church's confession and unambiguously present in the social policy of the General Assembly[3] (GA); (b) should clearly define the behavior and stance of the corporate entities whose policies or practices are at issue; and (c) should state the ends sought through divestment.
4. The decision should be taken after consultation with the ecumenical community, wherever possible. The implementation of a divestment action should ordinarily be in solidarity with other Christian bodies.

---

3. The General Assembly (GA) is the official gathering of the Presbyterian Church (USA) as national decision-making body.

5. Efforts should be made to examine the probable effects and consequences of the action with affected communities, particularly Presbyterians.

6. The proposed action should be sufficiently precise that the effect of its application can be evaluated.

7. Any proposed divestment action should include provision for: (a) informing appropriate church constituencies; (b) giving appropriate public visibility to the action; (c) engaging other governing bodies in advocacy for the ends that prompt divestment; and (d) giving pastoral care to the directly affected.[4]

The seven criteria above were used quite well in the Israel/Palestine divestment debate. Beginning in 2004 with a 431–62 vote, the General Assembly instructed MRTI to develop a "phased, selective divestment" process related to companies doing business in Israel. The goal was not blanket divestment, but rather to change corporate behavior. For years MRTI was tasked with utilizing the corporate engagement process to ensure that church investments were made in companies that pursued peace in Israel, the West Bank, Gaza, and East Jerusalem.

The 2006 General Assembly, recognizing potential harm and misunderstandings from the 2004 vote, made a slight course correction. They voted (483–28) to clarify language; the new resolution insisted on practical reality considerations and commitment to positive outcomes, and apologized for pain caused.[5] In addition, MRTI was directed to include divestment in its engagement process but only as a last resort.

The General Assembly in 2010 affirmed Israel's right to exist and, in typical Presbyterian fashion, also challenged human rights abuses, militarism, and any activity not grounded in justice, righteousness, and mercy. "On the basis of Christian principles and as a matter of social witness" (219th General Assembly 2010), the Committee on MRTI then was asked to continue corporate engagement with companies profiting from the sale and use of their products for nonpeaceful purposes. The hope was that engagement would change egregious behavior inimical to church values.

In 2012, the GA approved the boycott of products developed in occupied Palestinian territories. It was not a boycott against Israeli products; it was a

---

4. 1984 GA Minutes of the 196th GA, Presbyterian Church (USA), May 29–June 6, 1984, accessed August 5, 2019, link & pp. *https://www.presbyterianmission.org/wp-content/uploads/Divestment-Strategy-PCUSA-1984.pdf*, pp. 8–9.

5. PCUSA FAQ on 2006 Divestment Overture, July 2006, accessed August 5, 2019, *https://www.pcusa.org/site_media/media/uploads/oga/publications/journal2006.pdf*, pp. 943–45.

call to recognize that factories in illegal settlements extended the occupation and prevented a just peace between Israel and Palestine. The Presbyterian Mission Agency and Foundation were directed in 2012 to make "positive investments" (see case study on the Colombian Presbyterian University) in Palestinian enterprises to help create a strong infrastructure. Investments were subsequently made in education, energy, and microfinance. This was in keeping with using investments as a means to promote justice.

While these actions by the Presbyterian Church (USA) did not bring peace to Israel/Palestine, they were faithful in using the Mission Responsibility Through Investment engagement process to endorse a two-state solution, reaffirm Israel's right to exist, encourage interfaith dialogue, promote positive investments, and improve lives of Israelis and Palestinians. As Matthew 25:40 states, "Truly I tell you, just as you did it to one of the least of these who are members of my family, you did it to me."

Other Denominational Reflections

Clearly, the Presbyterians went about their process in a very strategic and thoughtful way, reflecting the structure and procedures built into their denominational processes. It was not done rashly or quickly and allowed for significant consensus to be built over time, allowing for the maximum support within their denomination for the General Assembly's actions. However, this is just one example to show the importance of patience, collaboration, and strategic action incrementally over time with SRI. Like the Presbyterian process, most denominations have several similar committees, national gatherings, and processes that were created to enable vigorous discussion, which leads to decisive action. Instead of delving into more "behind-the-scenes" reviews of other denominational processes, we thought it would be valuable to focus more generally and to interview other denominational leaders about their reflections of their own processes and experiences over time.

Like the Presbyterian Church, the Episcopal Church was also an early leader in the SRI movement due to the actions taken against apartheid in South Africa in the early 1970s. As a bit of background, for the Episcopal Church the General Convention is its governing body, which meets every three years. "It is a bicameral legislature that includes the House of Deputies and the House of Bishops, composed of deputies and bishops from each diocese. During its triennial meeting deputies and bishops consider a wide range of important matters facing the Church. In the interim between triennial meetings, various committees, commissions, agencies, boards and task forces created by the General Convention meet to implement the decisions and carry on the work of the General Convention."[6]

SRI actions of the Episcopal Church's General Convention have been well reported. So we thought it would be valuable to ask one of the Church's main leaders about his perspectives on this very broad topic. We greatly appreciate that Kurt Barnes, treasurer of the Episcopal Church, was willing to correspond with us about a number of issues related to the denomination and his views on topics involving SRI.[7] Clearly there has been much collaboration among Episcopal Church leaders as well as incremental decision-making and discussion on these issues over many decades. We posed the following to Kurt: "The Episcopal Church (also known as DFMS or the Domestic and Foreign Mission Society of the Protestant Episcopal Church) is considered a trailblazer by many, due to its actions regarding apartheid in the early 1970s. How do you see the current efforts of the Episcopal Church connecting with its historic activity in this area?"

Kurt responded: "I always hope the Church will remember the past but adapt to the present and future. The Episcopal Church was a founding member of the Interfaith Center for Corporate Responsibility and remains a member. Its socially responsible investing continues to follow a trinity of advocacy, affirmative investing, and, to a lesser extent, avoidance. In 2018 and 2019, the DFMS has served as lead or cosponsor of shareholder resolutions with twelve US companies on subjects of human rights, fossil fuel emissions, human trafficking, and gun safety. During 2019, we will engage twenty-five companies through dialogues, resolutions, and letter writing. Boycotts were effective in several instances in the 1970s, but corporate engagement—being at the table—is key to achieving lasting change in policy."

We also dug deeper on divestment and engagement with Kurt by asking: "There have been significant discussions around fossil fuel divestment over the years and more recently choosing NOT to divest from certain companies and industries so as to retain a seat at the table with companies. How does the Episcopal Church balance these issues with its own fiduciary responsibilities? Also, how have the incremental processes of committee work and open discussion benefited the Episcopal Church and its ability to ensure various

---

6. "About the General Convention," The General Convention of the Episcopal Church, accessed June 12, 2019, *https://www.generalconvention.org/about-the-general-convention*.

7. Kurt Barnes, e-mail correspondence with authors, June 14, 2019.

voices are heard and that there will remain a balance between 'National Church' decisions and regional choices?"

Kurt responded: "TEC tries to engage in conversations with companies whose policies or products are not in agreement with the Episcopal Church's policies and beliefs. In response to General Convention resolution C045 (2015) regarding Episcopal Church investment in fossil fuels, the Executive Council Investment Committee (ECIC) adopted the guidelines summarized below.

1. No additional direct purchases of fossil fuel holdings;
2. Screen out all securities where a company reports that more than 10 percent of its revenue is derived from oil and gas (and create a list of prohibited names);
3. Convert any commingled/mutual fund holding to a socially responsible version, if available;
4. Consider investment managers that provide alternative energy themes.

". . . Maintaining a modest exposure to fossil fuel companies will enable the church to continue its active role of corporate engagement and proxy voting."

Engagement is clearly important to the Episcopal Church, so we inquired of Kurt, "Regarding the power of engagement with companies, how do you see the future of influencing policies, such as gun availability and gun control?" Kurt replied, "Again, lasting change generally results from persuasive conversation and shared interests."

Finally, we asked, "Clearly collaboration is key among the many leaders within the Episcopal Church. What did you see as the best example of this regarding socially responsible investing?" Kurt replied: "Actions regarding gun safety. First a few bishops calling attention to gun violence. Then taking it to the street in a march in Salt Lake City at General Convention 2015, they expanded awareness and participation among lay Episcopalians. Then at General Convention 2018, a resolution was approved overwhelmingly by both the House of Bishops and the House of Deputies endorsing the purchase of shares of gun manufacturers in order to engage those companies in conversations. Again, not boycott, divestment, or sanction, but *engagement*."

It was encouraging to see that the Episcopal Church remains so actively engaged in a movement that it helped foster in the early 1970s through its stand against apartheid even into today in its important and proactive actions.

As previously noted in another case study and other chapters, United Church Funds (UCF) is the foundation serving the needs of congregations and entities of the United Church of Christ (UCC). We corresponded with Katie McCloskey of UCF, and also a contributing author to this book, about UCF's experiences through the years working on behalf of their denomination.[8] We posed to Katie the following question: "The UCC has been able to do some wonderful work in the SRI space and has been very active through the ICCR and in many other ways for many years. Of its many accomplishments, what is UCF most proud of?"

Katie replied: "UCF is probably most proud of its constant state of listening and adapting as the UCC turned its concerns to different issues and as general understanding of SRI norms changed. UCF has never dismissed out of hand calls for investment changes or divestments from our stakeholders in the UCC—we've sought to keep an open mind and determine the feasibility of any particular call. When it wasn't possible to completely fulfill a call for divestment, we thought of other ways to adhere to the spirit of concern: when fossil fuel divestment was a priority of the denomination, we were able to create a divested fund for those institutions that wanted to act quickly. In the rest of our funds, we committed to periodically reviewing the appropriateness of maintaining our fossil fuel positions. Similarly, as the socially responsible investing industry grows and matures, UCF is proud that we have not limited ourselves to one aspect of the field. We keep evolving. We have added thoughtful ESG managers to our investment lineup, changed our exclusionary screens as the denomination updated its thoughts about acceptable practices and industries, and added thematic funds strategically. Now we're extremely excited to offer an impact-first fund, which will seek to fund solutions to global development needs, including financial inclusion for women and people of color, efficient energy provision to the global South, and healthy outcomes for communities. The Just World Fund is a fixed-income fund that will be available to faith-based institutions to invest in a way that is more inclusive than other opportunities for impact investing."

As a follow-up, we asked Katie: "What does UCF see as the best first step for congregations seeking to bring an SRI issue up to a national audience?" Katie replied: "In 2015, when a UCC conference minister intended to bring the call for fossil fuel divestment to the General Synod (the UCC biannual denomination-wide business assembly), he first contacted those

---

8. Katie McCloskey, e-mail correspondence with authors, June 17, 2019.

financial ministries that were going to be most impacted by the resolution he was drafting. This outreach, and the conference minister's request for negotiations before the resolution was introduced to the General Synod delegates, strengthened the resolution, and therefore made it more actionable for United Church Funds. Unlike in previous calls for divestment or SRI changes, UCF was able to suggest precise language that accurately represented the way we invest and the way changes would be accomplished. Seeking the advice and input from impacted stakeholders, including financial ministries, is an important way to strengthen any congregation's SRI concern."

Intrigued by UCF's answer to these two questions, we also reached out to the Disciples of Christ's Christian Church Foundation and asked the same questions to their Rev. Maggie Archibald.[9] "Of its many accomplishments, what is CCF most proud of?" The Rev. Archibald's response: "Throughout our sixty-year history, the Christian Church Foundation has been able to provide a prophetic witness across the life of the whole church without breaching our fiduciary responsibility. This stems from a belief that fiduciary responsibility and prophetic witness are not in conflict with each other but, instead, are complimentary to each other. This complimentary relationship has become especially true as SRI issues have grown in importance to companies' long-term sustainability and economic engine."

When we asked her, "What does CCF see as the best first step for congregations seeking to bring an SRI issue up to a national audience in the future?" she replied: "The Christian Church Foundation would encourage every congregation to start where they are by using the greatest resource they have available to them—their members. Members of your congregation work in different fields, have different connections within your community, and are more directly aware of the operations of the companies and organizations with which they work. These people are more conscious of the specific needs and immediate actions which can be taken to create change for good in your community and in the world."

So many perspectives and so many accomplishments! How would your denomination answer these same questions? Do you know the process your denomination has for raising new issues and how you could become more involved in SRI within your national discussions? The choices are yours to reflect upon, and the appropriate actions are yours to discern.

---

9. The Rev. Maggie Archibald, e-mail correspondence with authors, June 17, 2019.

Positive Investment Overview: Reformed University in Colombia*

Greg Rousos

The Presbyterian Church (USA) has a long-standing history of active investments that focus on positive social return. Investments in initiatives with positive social return typically involve more risk, as the investments are made in areas that are economically challenged. One would normally think that investments with more risk would offer a higher potential financial return. Due to the church's missional objective and desire to initiate positive social change in challenging areas, the investments offer lower financial return, but that lower financial return provides the beneficiary of the investment with the greatest opportunity for success by decreasing their cost of capital.

The Presbyterian Church's (USA) positive impact investment program is known as *creative investments*. The Creative Investment Program was implemented in 1975 by the 187th General Assembly as an answer to a charge presented to the United Presbyterian Church in the United States of America by the 183rd General Assembly in 1971.[1]

The Creative Investments Program focuses on areas including the self-development of people, development assistance, racial justice and racial ethnic ministries, equal rights for women and those marginalized in society, environmental justice, and quality of life assistance to the economically deprived. Since the inception of the program, tens of millions of dollars have been invested to promote positive social change.

---

* This material, including organizations and websites noted, is provided for informational purposes only and should not be viewed as an endorsement or as investment, tax, or other professional advice.

1. *The Corporate Witness of the General Assembly Presbyterian Church in the United States 1976*, approved by the 116th General Assembly of the Presbyterian Church in the United States and adopted by the General Assembly Mission Board on March 20, 1976, *https://www.presbyterianmission.org/wp-content/uploads/mrti_ga_policy_-_19761.pdf*.

Background

Education is foundational to addressing the concerns noted above. The CUR, Corporación Universitaria Reformada (University) of Barranquilla, Colombia, is an institution of higher education founded by the Presbyterian Church of Colombia and recognized by the Colombia National Ministry of Education since May 14, 2002. Despite only being in existence since 2002, the university already offers sixteen programs and has a growing number of students. The Presbyterian Church of Colombia founded the university and owns the properties, including the lots and buildings. The Presbyterian Church of Colombia also owns the Colegio Americano de Barranquilla, which is part of a network of kindergarten through twelfth grade schools throughout the country.

The university experienced rapid growth in the student body since 2011, when enrollment totaled only 254; enrollment is now exceeding 1,300. The university's motto is "Educate Life for Peace," which is of critical importance considering Colombia's current socioeconomic context, which includes narco-trafficking, paramilitary activity, and despair among young people. All of this takes place in a context of continuing armed conflicts, as peace accords only covered one of the two major guerrilla groups; peace talks are pending with the other group. As such, the university is focused on educating those with the least access to traditional university education. Over 70 percent of the students are from the lower economic strata in Colombia.

Over the years the university has evolved and developed new programs and curriculum. Much of the curricula focuses on reconciliation, forgiveness, and new ways of encountering others. The first schools included theology and psychology, but the university now includes more technically oriented curricula, such as accounting, business administration, engineering, and port and maritime administration. Today, the university offers three schools within the university, each with four academic degree programs. These include the following:

- social sciences, arts, and humanities, with degrees in psychology, theology, music, and Spanish/English education;
- economics, administration, and accounting sciences, with degrees in accounting, business administration, and maritime and port administration;
- engineering, with degrees in biomedical engineering, informatics, electromedicine engineering, and environmental engineering.

The university also provides one-year graduate certificate programs in international finance and organizational development. Overall, the university seems well positioned to respond to market and community needs and to develop future leaders.

A five-year development and strategic plan was launched in 2017, calling for the university to expand and become more involved in research and to expand its extension program. The university wanted to create more awareness across the region and enhance its reputation. To ensure long-term sustainability, the university was considering several initiatives, including rainwater management, solar energy, and increasing ties to the business sector. Many of these programs consider the academic level of most of the surrounding rural communities, which is somewhat analogous to continuing education programs or associate degrees offered by community colleges in the United States. This is an extremely valuable educational service to a much underserved population.

Positive Investment

The positive investment objective was to assist the university in overcoming a short-term shortfall in cash flow in recent years. Various governmental and economic changes and influences resulted in the university's financial challenges and adversely impacted its image. This resulted in declining enrollment, further complicating the university's financial position, and culminated in the university's requesting a loan several years ago.

The adverse impact to the university's financial situation threatened its long-term sustainability. The university, through Presbyterian USA world mission staff, reached out to ascertain if the Presbyterian Church (USA) might be able to assist during this financially challenging time. The Presbyterian Church (USA) was very familiar with the school and its good work.

At the request of denominational leadership, the Presbyterian Foundation engaged in discussions with the university to understand how the Foundation might best help them. The university requested a loan to avoid cancellation of critical programs and staff that could damage its reputation and its ability to serve the community. The Presbyterian Foundation understood the greatly needed services that the university provided to the community and those in Colombia, especially its focus on students with backgrounds that do not usually allow them access to a university education, and the university's focus on peace and reconciliation that is much needed in Colombia's current challenging economic and political context.

The Foundation conducted significant due diligence that included interviewing board members and management, reviewing business plans, analyzing financial statements and projections, and understanding mission alignment with the Presbyterian Church (USA). The Foundation also affirmed compliance with the Office of Foreign Asset Control lists and other regulatory requirements. After numerous meetings and document reviews, the Foundation determined that the university was a good candidate for a creative investment.

The Foundation and the university structured the creative investment as a loan for USD 300,000. The purpose of the loan was to allow the university to be maintained through the short-term financial crisis. The loan was structured with a grace period where no payments were due for a considerable period of time and with a very low interest rate. The grace period was designed to allow the university to stabilize its finances and programs.

Dennis Smith, the Presbyterian Church (USA) regional liaison for South America, noted that "The Presbyterian Church (USA) has been part of God's mission to the whole world for 180 years. From the very earliest days, one focus of this mission has been on education. For example, the American School of Bogotá, a ministry of the Presbyterian Church of Colombia, was established by PC (USA) missionaries 150 years ago. That focus on education illustrates our commitment to human dignity. We have understood that people of goodwill must do their homework, learn from the human experience, and act thoughtfully in their community seeking the common good. For the Presbyterian Foundation to invest in CUR at this critical time is very much in keeping with this tradition."

Positive Investment Benefits

The creative investment with the university provided numerous benefits to the school, its students, and its community. The creative investment continued important educational programs that stimulate economic activity and develop future leaders for the community and Colombia.

As part of the creative investment, the university decided to add and upgrade its technology. The school invested in new computer labs and technology infrastructure. The technology improvements have created positive awareness and have aided the university in attracting additional students. Further, the creative investment ensured that important professors and administrative personnel were retained. Due to this creative investment, the administration of the university is now confident in its ability to overcome this current shortfall, as it was recently given accreditation for several engineering disciplines and continues to develop relationships with international higher education partners.

As noted previously, the stability assured by this creative investment has allowed the university to develop strategic plans and goals. Enrollment has grown since the time of the loan and now exceeds 1,300. The university's strategic plan calls for an increase in enrollment to well over 3,000 by 2021, with significant growth in the schools of social sciences, arts, business, and engineering. The plan includes a commitment to marketing to improve awareness and grow enrollment. The marketing plan includes tactics focused on social media as well as more traditional tactics that include driving through neighborhoods and speaking through a megaphone promoting the university.

While the university benefited from a short-term influx of capital via a creative investment loan, the Presbyterian Church (USA) has benefited from the Presbyterian Church of Colombia in countless ways. The creative investment provides tangible proof of the commitment the Presbyterian Church (USA) has to the Presbyterian Church of Colombia. This commitment is demonstrated by supporting the people of Colombia and investing in their future. The creative investment provides funding for a foundational requirement of all communities and countries: education. Finally, the creative investment provides support to their partners in ministry, the Presbyterian Church of Colombia, during a critical time and demonstrates how positive investment can benefit and promote people, community, and country.

Sustainable Financing*

*Patricia Daly****

Leading up to the COP 21, the Paris Climate Agreement, my Dominican Sisters throughout the United States entered into a faith/praxis process: to study the issue of global warming, to hear from our Sisters in various parts of the country about their experiences of climate change, and to reflect theologically on the issue and offer ways that we can respond. We facilitated this with a DVD that can be used in any faith community: *Global Climate Change and the Praxis Cycle: A Production of the Earth Council of the Dominican Sisters in Committed Collaboration.* In the weeks before the Paris Agreement was finalized in 2015, each individual Congregation of Sisters of St. Dominic in the United States committed to pursue investments in the greenhouse gas (GHG) emissions-free economy. The Sisters who committed to this had one proviso: the investments also needed to focus on the UN Sustainable Development Goals.[1] The next challenge was to find a practical way to do this.

A Climate Finance Taskforce was appointed among the group, and members began to research options and reach out to investment firms to find products that would offer us this integration. After a few months, the Sisters found inspiring people who were trying to respond to this investment need, but in the end, there were no appropriate products offering these priorities. Knowledgable of the Interfaith Center on Corporate Responsibilty's (ICCR) engagement with large financial institutions, the Sisters turned to two companies that had initiated a sustainable finance/impact investment division.

---

* This material, including organizations and websites noted, is provided for informational purposes only and should not be viewed as an endorsement or as investment, tax, or other professional advice.

** Editor's note: This case study is a personal recap of how a Roman Catholic Order of Dominican Sisters, led by Sr. Patricia Daly, OP, was inspired to collaborate with a secular institution to create opportunities for investing in climate solutions that integrated the UN Sustainable Development Goals, thus enabling others to participate in those efforts.

1. "About the Sustainable Development Goals," United Nations, accessed May 31, 2019, *https://www.un.org/sustainabledevelopment/sustainable-development-goals/*.

Investments of this kind are designed to consider various socially responsible endeavors, while also looking for market rate returns. After months of meetings, one company was selected. This may have been one of the few times that a financial management firm actually worked with a client to develop new investment products for both the public and private space. Those funds were launched in 2018, and we are now monitoring those impact investments focused on climate solutions that integrate the UN Sustainable Development Goals. What might your efforts achieve in time?

For more information, please contact Sister Patricia Daly, OP, at patdalyop @gmail.com.

A Reflection on Mission-Based, Faith-Based Investing at The Riverside Church, NYC*

*Lisa Hinds***

Our God, the divine creator and master architect of the universe, would have made a pretty great portfolio manager. God's portfolio would be pure and just and clean and, moreover, bring offense to no one. Modern portfolio theory, even with all its complexity and mathematically proven analyses, could never grasp the enormity of our God's ability to maximize returns. Luckily, God chose another line of work.

Maybe that's a good thing. Maybe it's by design that our God would task and empower her hopelessly flawed, limited, self-absorbed human creation to be market participants together, without her divine thumb on the scale. The fight for alpha (outperforming the market) is fair that way. But what if some of those market participants are disciples of Jesus? Are we necessarily abiding by the same rules? Are we bound by a different code of behavior? Can we access the same markets in the same way? Are the outcomes we seek somehow different? And importantly, within an institutional investment framework, can we still afford to have nice things?

For disciples of Jesus, stewardship, or the discretionary control over long-term assets within an institutional framework, may take on a new and arguably higher meaning. At The Riverside Church in the City of New York (TRC), where I served as deacon and trustee for the six-year term ending in May 2018, I was honored to be able to step passionately into this purpose-

---

* This material, including organizations and websites noted, is provided for informational purposes only and should not be viewed as an endorsement or as investment, tax, or other professional advice.

** Editor's note: Please note, even this incredible congregation struggled with the "how" and the "what" in their discussions. Your congregation/organization may not be able to do all that The Riverside Church has done, but you, too, can act, as is appropriate for your context, both decisively and incrementally too.

driven role. Leading Riverside's finance committee (FC) as well as the church's ~$150 million endowment portfolio created an opportunity to seek God's power and provision; to discern and articulate the vision of a comprehensive faith-based investing plan; and to execute on that plan prudently and courageously. Our goal was clear: to support the mission of the church and its spending policy and to protect and grow the endowment, thus creating intergenerational value.

Riverside is an interdenominational, interracial, international, open, welcoming, and affirming church and congregation. All are welcome. But more so than these central, sometimes abstract, tenets, we are a community of actors. Our willingness and ability to make tangible the gospel (i.e., to take concrete steps to put our radical love for Jesus Christ into action) is who we have been called to be, not just because we have been blessed with a magnificent temple and a healthy endowment and have loud economic voices, but also because of a vibrant tradition of social justice activism. Riverside's prayer vigils, sit-ins, proclamations, and protest marches have been transformational in the civil rights era and beyond. But as a practitioner and active participant in capital markets, economics is where real change often begins. As an investment committee, "making tangible" necessarily took the form of portfolio construction, both tactical and strategic.

For starters, though, we recognized that as both fiduciaries and disciples, we had to establish a foundational belief system that would fully embrace our unique identity as well as our call to honor God, do justice, and drive the returns that would build his kingdom. We stood on Matthew 25:14–30, the parable of the talents, recognizing that capital has a moral responsibility to underwrite risk. And with that came three additional sets of duties for the investment committee:

1. To be authentic with the execution of our SRI (socially responsible investment) priorities;
2. To manage risk prudently;
3. To distinguish quantitatively and definitively between two disparate notions: charity and justice.

Item 2 above is critical to any investment committee that seeks a sustainable, responsible, professionally managed investment program. While there are volumes of academic materials written on risk management and plenty of ways to deconstruct, measure, and mitigate traditional and alternative forms of portfolio risk, our response was simple and consistent: "What could go wrong?"

Item 3 above may seem elementary or even presumptive: charity and investments are not to be conflated. Yet the committee was often asked to underwrite programs, resources, and other non-interest-bearing debt instruments that would create no financial return for the church. While there are ways of including such investments (possibly through a structured product) in a balanced portfolio, the committee had to maintain its focus on investments that would seek (at a minimum) a market rate of return. This underscores the importance of church governance and a structurally sound and conflict-free investment committee with well-documented policies and procedures.

Item 1 above—authenticity—is where things got messy. Regardless, we were committed to approaching this exercise as a spiritual discipline. Discerning our socially responsible investing priorities, and even defining what a social evil is, required a deeply rooted exercise in identity, character, and purpose. The question we put to the congregation was simple: "What kind of products, services, and industries are antithetical to our mission?" The ensuing debate was as introspective as it was defining. Our rich diversity and "open mic" culture created layers of complexity and awareness, even unearthing the warriors within. (Lesson learned: maybe make this question multiple choice, not short-answer essay!) These were exciting times of renewal and resurgence for both the community and for the newly elected finance committee chair who, in the end, could craft only imperfect solutions to some of the world's great challenges: (1) diversity and inclusion, (2) mass incarceration, and (3) environmental justice.

Diversity and Inclusion

Situation: The Riverside Church has 1,750 members and affiliates from more than 40 denominational, national, ethnic, and cultural backgrounds. Diversity rests at the core of our being. We believe that better decisions are made by different voices—of all genders, from different cultural/ethnic backgrounds who bring different perspectives and different life experiences—and when all those voices are heard and valued. Not surprisingly, the global investment management industry is one of the most unequal. "Firms owned by women and minorities manage a mere 1.3 percent of the investment industry's $69 trillion in assets."[1] Prior to 2012, all TRC asset managers were white males.

---

1. Julie Segal, "Asset Managers Owned by Women and Minorities Have to Work 10x as Hard for Assets," *Institutional Investor*, June 28, 2019.

Action: Active engagement with our investment managers, partners, advisors, custodians, administrators, etc. on issues of diversity and inclusion was a critical first step. Many were open to the discourse. Still others had no idea what we were talking about. When the response from a bewildered counterparty went something like "I'm not sure I know what you mean," we then rested on the gospel, using the opportunity to explain, teach, and make it relevant. We further made the dialogue even more provocative and challenging by distinguishing between under-represented minorities and over-represented minorities in the asset management industry. That's where things really got interesting!

Result: The outcome was that an RFP (request for proposal) was issued publicly and broadly to source investment partners who more credibly demonstrated the ability to deliver diverse talent. A key metric on the scorecard for each of the thirty-plus respondents clearly identified diversity and inclusion as a key success factor. Though the incumbent was invited to rebid, this particular relationship was ultimately terminated. Both the RFP and the scorecard in the search were used as models for other similarly situated endowment plans.

While all TRC vendors are accountable for substantive organizational diversity, currently more than 40 percent of the asset managers in the TRC portfolio are owned and/or controlled by under-represented minorities and/or women. The TRC portfolio has consistently ranked as a top-quartile performer (as ranked by similar endowments/foundations) over the last five consecutive fiscal years!

Mass Incarceration

Situation: Through such scholarly works as Michelle Alexander's *The New Jim Crow: Mass Incarceration in the Age of Colorblindness*, Douglas Blackmon's *Slavery by Another Name*, and Bryan Stevenson's *Just Mercy: A Story of Justice and Redemption*, we were offered compelling evidence of the inextricable link between mass incarceration and racial bias. We believed the issue to be both systemic and abhorrent. With the explosive rise in inmate populations, particularly for incarcerated children, our community felt resolute that mass incarceration may well define us as a society the way slavery once did. Recall that slavery wasn't deemed a crisis until the abolitionists made it one. "America's new shame" needed to be tackled.

Riverside had already locked arms on criminal justice reform; Riverside's dedicated Coming Home Ministry, which seeks to empower men and women who are returning to the community from incarceration, was well into its twentieth year of service. The finance committee believed it had no choice but to join the fight somehow. As always, the first step was to gather the facts and deconstruct the issue(s); given the limitations of David's slingshot, we had to make every attempt to target the *right* Goliath. Careful examination of every holding of each of our asset managers exposed utterly terrifying results: 13F SEC filings as of June 30, 2015, revealed that our highest performing asset manager held over 38 million shares (or ~$1.3 billion) of the largest private prison in America. Shareholder activism quickly became both our privilege and our burden.

Action: Societal transformation hardly ever happens without a market-driven transformation. The committee decided that both divestment and reinvestment were appropriate measures. Finding no off-the-shelf investable strategy that would proactively address this societal ill, The Riverside Church originated and structured its own unique and branded investment vehicle, Progress-Urban Strategy, to directly address recidivism and its root causes. By underwriting urban/small businesses committed to policies of "open door" hiring, we would be solving two persistent race-based inequities: (1) the inability of minority business owners to access growth capital and business services, and (2) the inability of formerly incarcerated people to secure legitimate, full-time employment. Open door hiring is an employment policy that does not consider its applicants' prior state of incarceration, drug abuse, or homelessness.

Result: The outcome created ancillary benefits that we had never imagined. First, the committee's move to immediately exclude all private prisons from its investment holdings was swift and clear and came with rousing congregational support. Second, the publicity around both divestment and the newly formed investment vehicle generated public conversation regarding investment in private prisons. It not only highlighted the unconscionable circumstances behind America's prison walls but also deconstructed the revenue model and the value chain within the industry. Riverside's engagement on this topic may have encouraged other asset managers to consider screening out various private prison stocks. While it is difficult to determine whether the eventual underperformance of the stock led to its institutional sell-off or vice versa, we were ultimately pleased with the result.

As the loan portfolio in the Progress-Urban Strategy is being built, returns on the fund have not yet been harvested.

Environmental Justice

Situation: Citing volumes of irrefutable scientific studies on climate change and impressive congregational support for bold and immediate action, the finance committee was called upon to respond and, as always, to act justly. To be clear, there was no debate as to the legitimacy of the science and humankind's role in the warming of the earth. The science was reliable: all things are connected. While love is the unifying theme of our faith, the precise biblical context in support of environmental justice rested on Genesis, specifically our command to be caretakers of the earth. Further, evidence was presented on the disproportionate effects of climate change on the poor and most vulnerable. This aligned squarely with our identity.

Action: In response to a call for institutional divestment from the fossil fuels industry, the finance committee (FC) prepared a comprehensive analysis that addressed the single issue of environmental justice and the FC's policy and tactical response to climate change. It was intended to:

1. Present context for how TRC's finance committee acts as fiduciary over the church's portfolio while incorporating core principles of environmental justice;
2. Discuss the finance committee's criteria to divest or reinvest or become "activist" in a specific company or industry group;
3. Provide detail into how TRC's finance committee has reflected and continues to reflect the collective belief system of its community in portfolio construction;
4. Offer perspective on the opportunity set before us with asset managers and specific environmentally based transactions; and
5. Highlight the body of work the finance committee has engaged in with our partners and friends in faith-based and mission-based investment teams.

As the paper included the proprietary intellectual capital of counterparties and partners, shared with the FC under nondisclosure agreements, distribution was limited. An excerpt is below.

How Is the Role of Fiduciary Defined?

Ultimately as fiduciaries, the FC is responsible for prudent stewardship over TRC's financial assets. Blessed with a portfolio seeded by our founders over 85 years ago, returns on invested capital are the primary source of revenue for the church and for the building of God's Kingdom. First and foremost, our task is to drive and protect the value of the portfolio.

. . . The Riverside Church has a long tradition of investing for impact within its portfolio. ESG (environmental social governance) factors are applied to create value, to generate returns, and to express our moral and ethical views. While there are a variety of ways to approach the discipline, an impact investment must have the following characteristics: (1) It has to have specific intent; (2) it has to be measurable/definable; (3) it has to offer a market rate of return. The finance committee is committed to identifying a best-in-class approach to impact investing. In summary, then, there is no ambivalence with how we invest. TRC seeks both a financial return and a social return and sees no competitive tension between the two.

How Is a Belief System Captured in an Institutional Investment Strategy?

The FC is aware that mission-based investors face headline risk as well as the risk of their investments undermining the work they are striving to do. In a perfect world, the TRC portfolio would align with the values and belief system of the community it serves; it would be a clear reflection of God's love and Her interpretation of a just society. Alas, the world is perfectly imperfect. Even holding the seemingly harmless T-Bill presents a serious paradox for our firearm exclusion.

Among the questions with which the FC grapples: How does purchasing shares in a company (actively or passively) reflect our identity? How do we craft new sets of criteria as new evil emerges? Our thinking has evolved considerably, as our learning has granted us new perspectives on our approach to the broader portfolio. When the issue of Ferguson, Missouri, arose in 2014, it was not a question of should we attend to these issues but rather how we should address them. Responsible stewardship over God's creation is just as core to our belief system. We have found more levers for advancing outcomes within our investment strategy.

We see power in our role as: (1) an asset owner who can dictate how our capital is allocated, (2) a customer of financial services with the capacity to request new approaches or products, (3) a shareholder who can vote proxies and request better ESG transparency from companies; and (4) a peer investor who can work with other institutional investors for a better regulatory framework at the SEC, or collaborate with other foundations on deals. So while our endeavor may have started with a keen focus on a subset of our endowment, this approach has seeped into our overall investment thinking.

How Do We (Will We) Execute?

Following the valiant leadership of members to mobilize our community into collective action, the FC has expended considerable resources in sourcing, discovering, diligencing, and underwriting the most prudent fund managers and direct transactions that would appropriately reflect our nuanced goal to reinvest in transitional and renewable energy sources. . . .

The FC further believes that TRC should continue to be a pillar of leadership on the issue of justice-based investing. Working collaboratively with our neighbors at Union Theological Seminary (UTS), Jewish Theological Seminary (JTS), United Church Funds (UCF), and the Interfaith Center on Corporate Responsibility (ICCR) has inspired systemic consideration of relevant and material ESG issues and has driven a higher standard for faith-based investors. Leveraging the talents and expertise of nonprofit organizations dedicated to mobilizing capital to drive social progress like SocialFinance.org has not only lent support to the issue but led it. None of this cognitive capture would be achievable without authentic collaboration, imagination, and openness.

In summary then:

- While there is justice deeply embedded in the TRC portfolio, the FC seeks to do even more. Environmental justice is just one single component of its comprehensive plan.

- The FC is comprised of competent, capable industry practitioners who seek first to serve God and the TRC community through word and witness.

- Investing for the sustainable future has the potential to lead to greater outperformance than divesting from carbon or environmentally intensive industries.

- Proactive reinvestment in renewable and transitional energy sources should be key to a purposeful, progressive, and impactful plan.

Result: A manager dedicated to "green real estate" was funded, demonstrating a proactive position and creating significant exposure to sustainability within the portfolio. The focus of the strategy was to adhere to sound real estate fundamentals and then tactically and strategically augment asset cash flows by selecting, integrating, and optimizing green technologies at the asset level in a diversified commercial real estate portfolio. Green technologies are used and designed to reduce operating expenses; sustainability protocols are incorporated to improve risk management; and operating policies and procedures are implemented to enhance cash flows. TRC's investment in this strategy has yielded an annualized return of 3.6 percent.

A manager dedicated to social and environmental equity was also funded. The two fundamental principles that underlie its investment standards are: (1) the promotion of a society that values human dignity and (2) the enrichment of our natural environment. Core to the manager's belief system are that companies prosper in the long run when they respect their communities, protect the environment, produce safe and useful products, and treat workers, investors, and suppliers fairly. TRC's investment in this strategy has yielded an annualized return of 5.1 percent.

Still other impact funds dedicated to environmental justice, including green bonds, are being studied. Further, the church's move toward divestment, energy efficiency, and sustainability was announced on April 25, 2017.[2]

Most active investors in the SRI community recognize and seek the double bottom line of financial and social returns. Both are measurable. Both are relevant. Our communities must hold us accountable for the outcomes we seek. As a prophet, God calls on us to act. For those of us who are able to serve God by allocating capital, know these three things: (1) the capital markets can be and should be used as a tool to bring about social change; use your superpowers for good. (2) God's love doesn't seek value—it creates it. And (3) in God we trust; everyone else bring data!

---

2. The press release can be found here: "New Release: Riverside Church Moves to Divest on Eve of Climate March," The Riverside Church, April 25, 2017, *https://www.trcnyc.org/news-divest/*.

Introduction to Resources/Appendix

James W. Murphy

The main goal of this book's appendix is to offer resources from multiple denominations and secular tools to assist you in your initial efforts to get started on considering how socially responsible investing might work for your congregation or organization. Some readers of this book will find their denomination's resources listed in the appendix, but unfortunately many will not. If yours is not listed, your denomination was not actively excluded—please do reach out to your denomination for further resources to assist in your efforts. Fortunately, as this is a growing area of interest for many, we expect there will be many more resources available in the future for congregations, religious organizations, and individuals.

Please do consider reaching out to your denomination's resources first. Many of the authors in this book work long hours and travel thousands of miles every year, while being paid much less than we would earn in comparable secular roles, all to ensure that the best possible investment, planned giving, and other resources are available to our beloved congregations and denominational institutions. These denominational resources exist to support your congregations/organizations and their members, and they do so with a deep conviction for the future of our various churches.

Wishing all of you every blessing as you continue on this journey!

Samples of Investment Policy Statements*

Sample IPS 1: Presbyterian Foundation

If you are a congregation or organization in the Presbyterian Church (USA) and would like additional resources or more customized endowment documentation, please contact the Presbyterian Foundation at (800) 858-6127 or visit their website at www.presbyterianfoundation.org for these resources and much more.

Client:

Pool or Account Name: Permanent Endowment Fund

Account Number:

Investment Policy Statement   Date: January 1, 20XX

I. Financial/Investment Objectives:

- The primary financial objectives of the Fund are to:

  - support a stream of regular distributions in support of annual budgetary needs; and

  - preserve the real (inflation-adjusted) purchasing power of the Fund net of regular distributions.

- In order to achieve the financial objectives, the Fund will target a real total annualized return of at least X.XX%, net of investment expenses, on average, over a five- to seven-year period.

- Diversify the portfolio across multiple sub-asset classes.

- Maintain appropriate levels of liquidity to meet three months of expected cash flows.

---

* Editor's note: As a reference, we have included two sample investment policy statements (IPS). You can also find many samples online, but we recommend that you reach out to your denomination or your denominational foundation for similar "template" documents for use in your specific context. The first sample is from the Presbyterian Foundation and the second is from the Episcopal Church Foundation. Congregations and organizations from these denominations may contact these foundations for direct assistance with editing these documents and to receive additional documents and materials that are also recommended.

Before your congregation/organization finalizes any investment decision, please seek the asisstance of appropriate financial and investment advisors, such as provided from your denomination or denominational foundation.

II. Guidelines and Parameters:

- Tax Exemption: The Fund is a tax-exempt fund that is qualified under Section 501(c)(3) of the Internal Revenue Code of 1986 (the "Code"). As such, those responsible for the Fund are required to adhere to the requirements of the Code, as amended from time to time to maintain such qualification.

- Responsible Investing: The Fund is invested in accordance with social witness principles. These principles include . . .

- Distribution Policy: Distribution Policy encompasses Spending Policy and administration fees. The distribution for each fiscal year will be determined by the Spending Policy. As of <<DATE>>, the current Spending Policy is X.XX% of the three/five-year moving average of quarterly valuations. For the management of the Endowment Fund, there is an annual administration fee of approximately X.XX% of the month-end valuation. Distributions are made monthly/quarterly.

- Prudent Management: Follow the Uniform Prudent Management of Institutional Funds Act (UPMIFA) for all funds.

- Account Type: <True> < Quasi> Endowment Fund

- Governing Law: <<State>> Note most states apply UPMIFA.

- Illiquidity Constraint: In order to manage consistently with the Valuation Policy, the Fund will have a maximum of 25% (based on current Net Asset Value [NAV]) of the portfolio allocated to illiquid private investment strategies (e.g., Private Equity, Venture Capital, Distressed, Natural Resources, Real Estate, and Timber).

- Annual Contributions: New gifts

- Performance Measurement: Total returns shall be compared to a weighted benchmark composite.

III. Targets:

Item	Level	Note
Target Return	X.XX%	X.XX% Spending and Administration plus X.XX% inflation
Volatility	XX%	Based on strategic allocation
Downside Exposure	-XX%	-5th percentile (2 standard deviations) outcome for one year

continued

Item	Level	Note
Beta to ACWI [All Country World Index]	X.X	Based on target allocation
Illiquidity Constraints	XX% (NAV); XX% (NAV + unfunded)	See illiquidity constraint note above
Manager Fee Budget	X.XX%	Weighted average across all managers
Target Volatility of Distributions	XX%	Volatility of stream of distributions
Spending Policy	X.XX% of XX quarter average of market value of Fund	Help support smoothing of distributions from Fund
Administration Fee	X.XX%	Fee recovered from Fund to provide for costs of administration

IV. Asset Allocation:

A. Asset Structure

The Fund's investments shall be diversified by manager, by asset class and investment strategy, and within asset classes. The purpose of diversification is to provide reasonable assurance that no manager, class of securities, or individual holding will have a disproportionate impact on the Fund's aggregate results.

The asset allocation of the Fund should reflect the proper balance for liquidity, preservation of purchasing power net of distributions, and risk tolerance.

Asset Class	Target	Range
Cash	X%	X% - X %
Intermediate Government Bonds	X%	X% - X%
Private Growth (Equity)	X%	X% - X%
US Equity	X%	X% - X%
Non US Equity	X%	X% - X%
Public Real Assets	X%	X% - X%
Hedge Funds	X%	X% - X%
Total	100%	

B. Asset Allocation Rebalancing Strategy

The portfolio's asset allocation will be analyzed quarterly. Portfolio rebalancing will generally be done when one or more asset classes develop a plus or minus variance from the target allocation greater than X%. Account specific income, short- and long-term capital gain or loss may warrant some leeway in executing the rebalancing strategy.

V. Investment and Administration Team:

Investment Officer

Relationship/Trust Officer

VI. Communications and Review Plan:

Statements	Quarterly
Investment Reviews	Annually
Performance Measurement	Quarterly
Online account viewing system	As needed

< > Officer

Date

Sample IPS 2: Episcopal Church Foundation (ECF)*

The sections below are excerpted from a longer, more comprehensive set of "best practice" Endowment and Gift Acceptance Policies, which ECF staff would be happy to share and adapt for use in any Episcopal parish. ECF also has customized documents for other institutions, schools, camp and conference centers, and of course, for dioceses. Please contact ECF at 800-697-2858 or by e-mail at endowment@episcopalfoundation.org for these resources and much more.

FOR THE ENDOWMENT AND INVESTMENT FUND
OF
ST. SWITHIN'S EPISCOPAL CHURCH
ANYTOWN, USA

SECTION A
Investment Policy Statement

Purpose

This Investment Policy Statement establishes the philosophy, guidelines, and investment objectives for managing the investments of the FUND.

Responsibility

The ultimate responsibility for managing the FUND resides with the Vestry, which has chosen to delegate portions of its responsibility to the COMMITTEE, which will administer the portfolio of the FUND in accordance with these guidelines, as adopted and amended from time to time. These guidelines shall be reviewed at least annually by the COMMITTEE to determine whether they should be amended or remain unchanged. The COMMITTEE may choose to employ an outside investment manager.

Objectives

The assets of the FUND are to be invested with the same care, skill, and diligence that a prudent investor would exercise in investing institutional endowment funds. The primary objective will be to provide a total return

---

* Before your congregation/organization finalizes any investment decision, please seek the asisstance of appropriate financial and investment advisors, such as provided from your denomination or denominational foundation.

commensurate with the Spending Rule Policy and achieve growth in principal to keep pace with inflation, net of all investment fees.

INVESTMENT GUIDELINES

Time Horizon

The FUND'S investment objectives and strategic asset allocation are based on a long-term time horizon.

Risk Tolerance

Because of its long-term time horizon, the FUND can tolerate some interim fluctuation in market value and rates of return in order to achieve its objectives. High-level risk, high volatility, and low-quality rated securities, however, are to be avoided.

Prohibited Investments

The COMMITTEE shall not invest in private placements, restricted stock or other illiquid issues, arbitrage, and other uncovered options, and shall not engage in short sales, margin transactions, or other similar specialized investment activities; however, the use of funds that use these investment activities in a constructive manner is permitted.

Socially Responsible Investing

The FUND is invested in accordance with social witness principles. These principles include . . .

Standard Asset Allocation and Diversification

The portfolio is to provide for long-term growth of principal and income without undue exposure to risk. The portfolio shall be invested in equities, fixed income securities, and cash equivalents based upon an acceptable asset mix that is conducive to participation in rising markets, while permitting adequate protection in falling markets. In addition, the investment mix will take into consideration the payout requirements to satisfy the annual draw, normally between 3% and 5% of the average market value of the twelve trailing quarters. Should there be a need to change the spending rate, the COMMITTEE will review the asset mix and the asset allocation. In addition, the target allocations should be reviewed at least annually by the COMMITTEE in conjunction with the investment manager(s) to reflect a prudent response to current market conditions.

The initial target asset allocation and ranges shall be as follows:

Asset Class	Low	Target	High
Equities	60%	70%	80%
Fixed/Cash	20%	30%	40%
Other	0%	0%	20%

The investment manager will be asked to consult with the COMMITTEE regarding the use of sub-asset classes and their initial strategic targets and ranges. The manager will then have the discretion to make asset allocation decisions within these ranges. The COMMITTEE will review these decisions quarterly. The grid below provides an example of sub-asset class targets and ranges.

Asset Class	Low	Target	High
US Large Cap	10	x	50
US Mid Cap	0	x	15
US Small Cap	0	x	15
International Developed	10	x	55
International Emerging Markets	0	x	20
REITS [Real Estate Investment Trusts]	0	x	25
Commodities	0	x	15
Investment Grade Fixed Income	10	x	40
Non-Investment Grade Fixed Income	0	x	15
International Emerging Market Fixed Income	0	x	10
Treasury Inflation Protected Securities	0	x	15
Cash	0	x	5

[The targets and ranges shown here are for illustration only. Please consult with your investment manager when establishing your long-term strategic targets and ranges based on current market conditions, time horizons, expected draws, risk tolerance, and other factors.]

Allocation of Responsibilities

The COMMITTEE, along with any and all fiduciaries, is responsible for ensuring that all assets are managed effectively and prudently. It is responsible for formulating overall financial objectives and investment standards of the FUND. Additionally, with respect to asset management, the COMMITTEE is responsible for:

- Allocating the assets among investment media that are deemed appropriate and prudent.
- Selecting and evaluating the performance of a qualified Trustee/Custodian, Investment Manager(s), and Investment Consultant, if applicable.
- Monitoring performance by means of regular reviews (no less than annually) to assure that objectives are being met and that standards are being followed.
- Taking appropriate action if objectives are not being met or if standards are not being followed.
- Communicating on a structured, ongoing basis with managers responsible for investment results.

The COMMITTEE shall meet at least semiannually and shall provide a written report to the Vestry.

Responsibilities of the CUSTODIAN

The Custodian is responsible for:

- Fulfilling all the regular fiduciary duties required of a Custodian/Trustee by pertinent state and federal laws and regulations.
- Safekeeping the assets of the Parish. Securities must be held by a Custodian/Trustee that is a reputable, well-established financial institution.
- Supplying timely reports of transactions and valuations of the assets.

Responsibilities of the INVESTMENT MANAGER(S)

The Investment Manager is responsible for:

- Designing an investment strategy within policies established by the COMMITTEE.
- Implementing security selection and timing within policy guideline limitations.

- Supplying timely written quarterly reports of investment performance results to the COMMITTEE.
- Meeting and/or communicating in writing with the COMMITTEE at least semiannually to review the performance and discuss current strategy.
- Notifying the COMMITTEE in writing of any material deviation from the stated investment approach.

Assets are to be managed in conformity with the stated investment guidelines unless, in the manager's opinion, to do so would clearly be imprudent. The Investment Manager(s) shall notify the COMMITTEE *in writing* immediately of any material deviations from the investment standards.

Monitoring Asset Allocation and Rebalancing

The Investment Manager(s) should review the asset allocation of the portfolio at least quarterly. The portfolio should be kept within +/-3% of the current tactical position of the portfolio.

Performance Measurement Guidelines

The primary measurement of performance will be benchmark-relative returns. However, providing protection against inflation is an additional goal where possible.

The following are the benchmarks to be used for performance measurement:

Asset Class	Benchmark
US Large Cap Equity	S&P 500 Index
US Mid Cap Equity	S&P MidCap 400 Index
US Small Cap Equity	Russell 2000 Index
International Developed Large Cap Equity	MSCI EAFE Index
International Developed Small Cap Equity	S&P EPAC SmallCap Index
International Emerging Markets Equity	MSCI Emerging Markets Index
US REITS	DJ US Select REIT Index
International REITS	DJ Global ex-US Select RE Securities Index
Commodities	Bloomberg Roll Select Comm Total Ret Index
US Fixed Income—Investment Grade	BCAP US Aggregate Bond Index
—Investment Grade Intermediate Term	BCAP US Intermediate Credit Bond Index

continued

Asset Class	Benchmark
—TIPS	BCAP US TIPS Index
—Non-Investment Grade	Bloomberg Barclays US High Yield Custom BB/B ex-144A Index
International Fixed Income	JPM EMBI Global Diversified Index

Each investment strategy will be measured against the benchmark listed above, and each portfolio will be measured against a blended benchmark, weighted based on the target asset allocation of each portfolio.

If the Investment Manager proposes an investment strategy that should be measured against a benchmark different from those listed above, the COMMITTEE must approve it.

SECTION B
Spending Policy

Money will be distributed from the FUND upon written request of the Vestry and with the approval of the COMMITTEE for those uses which conform to the purposes and restrictions established by donors or incorporated in the Enabling Resolution.

Funds available for distribution will be determined by using a total return principle, i.e., return derived from dividends and interest *as well as* realized and unrealized capital gains. The funds available for distribution during any one year will be limited to a percentage of the market value of the FUND that is based on a three-year rolling average, with measures taken at the end of each of the preceding twelve quarters. The market value for this purpose will be taken net of the fees for investment management.

The percentage of the FUND made available for distribution shall be determined each year by the COMMITTEE and will normally fall in the range of 3% to 5%. In so doing, market performance of the portfolio will be an important consideration. It will be the goal of the COMMITTEE to grow, or at least maintain, the purchasing power of the FUND, taking into account the impact of inflation and fees.

[*A disagreement between the Vestry and the Endowment Committee about the spending rate—should it be 3% or 5% of a rolling three-year average value—is not a dire emergency. Ultimately the Vestry decides if they will accept the Committee's recommendation or not. Note, however, that in some states the Uniform Prudent Management of Institutional Funds Act (UPMIFA) says that spending 7% is considered "imprudent." The goal of the Committee is to maintain the spending power of the endowment over time, considering factors such as the spending rate, inflation, fees, and what other nonprofits are spending. The Committee then invests in such a way as to achieve a rate of return equal to or greater than the annual draw plus inflation plus fees.*

Some churches use a five-year rolling average to smooth out the ups and downs of the market. Churches just starting out that do not have a multiyear average can apply the spending rate to one year's average value in the first year, then two years, and finally three (or five) years.]

Any unexpended funds from those available for distribution in a given year will be accrued and will continue to be considered available for distribution in subsequent years unless otherwise designated by action of the COMMITTEE with the approval of the Vestry. Expenses related to the management and administration of the FUND will be deducted from the funds available for distribution.

Types of Planned Gifts

	Bequest by Will	Pooled Income Fund	Charitable Gift Annuity	Charitable Remainder Unitrust	Revocable Trust	Life Estate
	Give assets through will	Give to fund, receive income payments for life	Annuity issued in exchange for property (usually cash or securities)	Irrevocable trust which pays an amount based on annual value of assets	Trust which donor can modify or terminate at later date	Give real estate but retain right to use it for life
Income to donor	None	Income for life Rate based on market conditions	Income for life, may be deferred Fixed rate based on donor's age at time of gift	Varying percentage based on investment conditions	All or portion of the net income	Retention of right to use property for income purposes
Frequency of payment		Usually quarterly	Usually quarterly	Usually quarterly	Frequent	
Tax deduction	Possible reduction of estate and inheritance taxes	Initial possible income tax reduction. Capital gains tax and death tax reductions	Initial possible income tax reduction. Partially taxexempt payments and possible reduction of death taxes	Initial income tax deduction. Possible reduction of estate and inheritance taxes. Avoid gains taxes if funded with appreciated securities.	Possible reduction of estate and inheritance taxes	Tax deduction based on equity in the property and donor's age. Possible death tax reductions
Special advantages	Can be designated	Satisfaction of making major gift while living	Satisfaction of making major gift while living	Satisfaction of making major gift while living	Managed, professional oversight of investments; avoid probate	Satisfaction of making major gift while living

continued

Source: The Episcopal Church Foundation, 475 Riverside Dr., Ste. 750, New York, NY 10115, (800) 697-2858. For more information: e-mail: Giving@EpiscopalFoundation.org or visit: *www.Episcopal Foundation.org.*

Types of Planned Gifts *continued*

	Life Insurance Gift	Charitable Lead Trust	Bargain Sale	Appreciated Property	Retirement Assets
	Assignment of policy to church or church owns policy on donor's life	Trust pays church income, returns remainder to donor, or gives remainder to heirs after set number of years	Sell asset to church at below-market price	Give assets that have appreciated in value while living	Give tax-deferred assets to a charity as a beneficiary at death
Income to donor	None	None	Purchased price of asset	None	None
Frequency of payment					
Tax deduction	Possible tax deduction of premiums and cash value of policy	Trust usually passes to heirs at reduced gift and death tax rates	Partial income tax deduction for amount "lost" by the sale	Income tax deduction; capital gains tax may be avoided	
Special advantages	Ability to "leverage" gift	Trust dissolves after set period of time (10 to 20 years)	Satisfaction of making major gift while living	Versatile—most any form of property could qualify	Charity receives assets without paying deferred taxes

Denominational Resources and Foundations

This section is clearly not inclusive of the many denominations which exist today. However, we include these references for your initial use. Please contact your own denomination for more resources.

American Baptist
American Baptist Foundation
www.abcofgiving.org

Socially responsible investing (SRI) reflects our American Baptist values, enabling investors and donors to participate in investment strategies that support their beliefs. American Baptist Foundation (ABF) adheres to the broad social screens adopted by American Baptist Churches USA, prohibiting investments in firms primarily involved in gambling, defense and weapons, tobacco, and alcohol. Additionally, ABF and our investment managers may implement additional screens from time to time. Under the direction of our finance committee, our investment consultants and money managers constantly review our holdings to help ensure that our investments satisfy our SRI mandates. While most ABF equity investments are in large stocks, there are also investments in some medium, small, and foreign company stocks. Ensuring that our investments satisfy social screens can be challenging; however, we have proven to be very capable in this area. ABF is considerate toward the social and environmental needs of our community, nation, and environment.

Church of the Brethren
Brethren Foundation Inc. (BFI) and Brethren Foundation Funds Inc. (BFFI)
www.cobbt.org/about-us-0

Brethren Foundation Inc. and Brethren Foundation Funds Inc. provide deferred gift and investment opportunities for members and organizations of the Church of the Brethren, as well as others who affirm Brethren Values Investing guidelines. BVI guidelines, which are based on positions of the Church of the Brethren as expressed by its Annual Conference action, exclude companies that generate 10 percent or more of their revenue from Department of Defense contracts, weapons and their components, abortion, alcoholic beverages, defense, gambling, tobacco, or pornography. Companies engaging in human rights violations, as well as consistent violators of environmental regulations, are also excluded. In addition, the twenty-five largest publicly traded US defense contractors are excluded. As shareholders, BFI and BFFI initiate and participate in shareholder engagement with corporations. BFFI also offers a Community Development Investment Fund through which organizations put their invested assets to work funding affordable housing, microlending, and other community development initiatives.

Community of Christ
www.cofchrist.org

Community of Christ offers member jurisdictions the option to pool funds for investment for the pursuit of operational and missional opportunities. The church is sensitive to the intent of World Conference resolutions, and the desire of membership to invest in companies with ethical environmental, social, and corporate governance practices. Community of Christ endeavors to invest in companies that demonstrate a high awareness of products and processes that are environmentally friendly, leave a minimal footprint, and promote sustainability; socially, they implement internationally recognized human rights standards; corporately, they uphold financial, social, and ethical governance structures. Community of Christ endeavors not to invest in companies that produce products or use processes that are toxic to the environment; manufacture defense industry equipment, such as armaments, weapons, or munitions; use child labor and sweatshops; or generate tobacco, alcohol, gaming, or pornography. We believe following these principles will help meet commitments to beneficiaries and better align our investment activities with the broader interests of society.

Disciples of Christ
Christian Church Foundation
www.christianchurchfoundation.org

The Christian Church Foundation helps achieve the vision of the Christian Church (Disciples of Christ) through planned giving, endowment funds, and other avenues through which donors can charitably distribute their gifts within the church and the world. The Christian Church Foundation works with individual donors and local congregations to determine their passion for ministry and discern together the best way they can use their gifts to support ministry. The Christian Church Foundation is a member of the Interfaith Center on Corporate Responsibility (ICCR) and engages with companies to be socially and environmentally responsible. Each of the Christian Church Foundation funds reflects the organization's dedication to socially responsible investing. The Bostick Select Fund, launched in 2019, upholds this commitment while excluding investments in fossil fuels, weapons manufacturers, and companies targeted for divestment because of their involvement in perpetuating the Israeli-Palestinian conflict. The goal of the Christian Church Foundation is to move money to mission while helping Disciples make a difference in the world.

Episcopal
Episcopal Church Foundation
www.episcopalfoundation.org

ECF partners with congregations, dioceses, and other Episcopal faith communities, empowering them to engage in strategic visioning and planning, develop effective lay and clergy leadership teams, and raise and manage financial resources for ministry, including capital campaigns, investment management, planned giving resources, and life income gift and donor-advised fund options. ECF's programs, products, and services help congregations respond to the changing needs of the Episcopal Church in the twenty-first century.

With nearly $400 million in investments from 300 clients, ECF has helped hundreds of Episcopal dioceses, churches, schools, and church-related organizations *organize, invest, and grow* their endowments and permanent funds. Our Endowment Management Solutions (EMS) program covers the complete spectrum of endowment needs, from starting an endowment fund, to updating endowment policies, to investing prudently, including socially responsible (SRI) and environmental, social, and governance (ESG) options, and guidance on spending wisely. ECF's commitment to responsible endowment management reflects our belief that endowments breathe new life into a congregation, make new ministries possible, spark creative outreach projects, and ease the burden of long-term capital expenses.

The Episcopal Church (*Domestic and Foreign Mission Society*)
Episcopal Church SRI site: *www.episcopalchurch.org/library/topics/socially-responsible-investing*.

Evangelical Lutheran Church in America
ELCA Foundation
www.ELCA.org/foundation

The ELCA Foundation, a ministry of the Evangelical Lutheran Church in America (ELCA), supports members and congregations with planned giving and endowment management services. Designed specifically for its congregations and affiliated ministries, the Endowment Fund Pooled Trust—Fund A allows for the collective long-term investment of funds and provides distributions to support ministries throughout the church and world.

Portico serves as the investment manager for multiple asset class portfolios within Fund A and, where possible, uses a socially responsible investing approach in these portfolios. This approach is in alignment with ELCA social teachings and policies and uses ELCA guidance on social criteria screens, shareholder advocacy (i.e., shareholder filings, proxy voting, dialogues), and where possible positive social investments (e.g., community economic development, companies taking steps toward a sustainable environment). The eight ELCA social criteria screens used include alcohol, environmental damage, gambling, military weapons, pornography, private prisons, tobacco, and human rights.

Lutheran Church—Missouri Synod
Lutheran Church—Missouri Synod Foundation
www.lcmsfoundation.org

The LCMS Foundation serves the 2-million-member Lutheran Church—Missouri Synod in two areas: helping church members to make estate gifts and assisting ministries with their investment needs. The Foundation utilizes an outside investment advisor and best-in-class fund managers to construct portfolios that are consistent with the goals of our donors and ministries. In managing over $800 million in assets entrusted to us by others, we seek to align the investment options we offer with the values of our church body.

The majority of the Foundation's fund managers utilize SRI/ESG factors as a component of their evaluation of potential investment opportunities. Additionally, we further screen our investments to exclude companies that participate directly in the production of abortifacients.

With sixty years serving the church and more than $1 billion in gifts distributed to ministries of the church during that time, the LCMS Foundation seeks to continue that legacy of assisting donors and ministries with spreading the gospel for generations to come, until Christ returns in glory.

Mennonite
Everence Foundation (formerly the Mennonite Foundation)
www.everence.com

Everence Foundation is part of the Everence family of financial services and has helped individuals, congregations, and organizations since 1952, offering gift plans and charitable services. As a donor-advised foundation, Everence Foundation is designed to make giving easier, more flexible, and as simple as possible. In 2018, donors contributed $49 million through Everence Charitable Services, and $59.6 million in distributions was made based on donor recommendations. A full range of charitable services are available that include donor-advised funds, charitable trusts and gift annuities, planned giving, legacy planning, and the use of values-driven and impact investments. At Everence, a stewardship ministry of Mennonite Church USA, generosity is an important part of developing and carrying out overall financial planning, helping individuals and institutions integrate their faith and finances.

Presbyterian Church (USA)
Presbyterian Foundation
www.presbyterianfoundation.org

A vital part of the Presbyterian Church (USA), the Presbyterian Foundation cultivates, attracts, and manages financial resources of individuals and institutions to further Christ's mission. We work to strengthen congregations and related mission and ministry efforts by developing gifts and managing funds on their behalf. We work with them to build communities of generosity among their members and constituents. Our team of dedicated ministry relations officers across the United States regularly visit churches and Mid Council organizations to partner with them, offering stewardship, planned giving, endowment, and many other resources that can help sustain mission and ministry until Christ comes again. Additionally, the Foundation's subsidiary, New Covenant Trust Company, provides a means for individuals, ministries, and congregations to invest in ways that are consistent with Presbyterian values. In all our work, we remain focused on the Reformed values that have guided our stewardship and investment for more than 200 years.

Religious Society of Friends (Quaker)
Friends Fiduciary Corporation
www.friendsfiduciary.org

Friends Fiduciary Corporation (FFC) is a Quaker nonprofit organization providing cost-effective, socially responsible investment management services exclusively to Quaker meetings, churches, schools, and organizations. FFC manages over $470 million for more than 390 constituent organizations across the country. We faithfully steward these assets in ways consistent with Quaker values. Friends Fiduciary is a manager of managers, selecting best-in-class investment managers who implement Quaker socially responsible investment criteria for specific asset classes. We are active investors in the companies we own, engaging in company dialogues, filing shareholder proposals, and voting proxies. We believe Quaker values are also good, long-term, sustainable business values, and we seek to witness to those values on Wall Street, both as a testament to our faith and to maximize the long-term value of our investments.

Roman Catholic

Depending on the legal structure of the Roman Catholic diocese, individual parishes may or may not be able to hold their own invested or endowed funds. Finance councils may check with their local diocese finance office regarding ways to participate in SRI/ESG. Larger Roman Catholic organizations oversee their own investments and SRI strategy, but smaller mission dioceses work with the well-known organization Catholic Extension (below), for their SRI investment and planned giving needs. You may also review the full description of the United States Conference of Catholic Bishops (USCCB) SRI guidelines at www.usccb. org/about/financial-reporting/socially-responsible-investment-guidelines.cfm.

Catholic Extension
www.catholicextension.org

Based in Chicago, Catholic Extension offers financial support to eighty-six under-resourced Roman Catholic mission dioceses throughout the United States. Through fundraising from individuals, we support the poorest places in this country, where faith communities face enormous hardships and rely heavily on their faith and their church to confront these challenges. Their faith reminds them that they are not alone and offers hope, confidence, and optimism to move ahead with their lives, against all odds. Through strategic investment initiatives available to mission dioceses and other Roman Catholic organizations, we are meeting the unique pastoral, operational, and financial needs of faith communities. Programs such as the Mission Diocese Fund, with over $150 million under management, multiply the impact of our donors' gifts while providing the opportunity for dioceses to access top-level investment funds that would otherwise be outside their financial capacity.

Unitarian Universalist Association (UUA)
www.uua.org/finance/investment

The Unitarian Universalist Common Endowment Fund (UUCEF) is available for the investment of endowment funds, trust funds, and other assets of Unitarian Universalist congregations and organizations that have a long-term investment perspective and the need for income to support their missions. Under oversight of the Unitarian Universalist Association (UUA) Board of Trustees, the Investment Committee selects professional outside advisors and investment managers utilizing criteria set forth in the UUA investment policies, which direct that investments be in alignment with UU values. The Fund brings investors an added dimension—an active program of Socially Responsible Investing (SRI), which consists of making investment decisions that reflect UU values and contribute to positive social and environmental change. The three main strategies of SRI are investment selection, shareholder engagement, and community investing. "Investment selection" means using social, environmental, and governance (ESG) criteria in selecting our investments and excluding companies that are incompatible. "Community investing" is directing a portion of our investments in a way that helps to ameliorate poverty and social inequality. And by "Engagement" we mean working to improve the environmental and social performance of the companies whose securities we own. The UUCEF gives UU congregations a powerful and wide-ranging impact on corporate behavior and other issues of deep concern to Unitarian Universalists. These SRI initiatives represent an effective way to bring UU ideals to the marketplace. Specifically, shareholder advocacy and proxy voting initiatives seek to give investors a way to have UU values represented and to change the behavior of US and multinational corporations.

United Church of Canada
The United Church of Canada Foundation
www.unitedchurchfoundation.ca

The United Church of Canada Foundation has always striven to ensure that our investments are consistent with both the values and mission of the Church and our fiduciary responsibilities as trustees. The national investment bodies of the United Church of Canada's Treasury, Pension Fund, and Foundation see the growing importance of responsible investing as affirmation of our belief that corporate responsibility and long-term performance are not mutually exclusive but are complementary. We embrace responsible investment (RI) because it reflects our central goal of providing returns aligned with values.

The national investment bodies are signatories and/or members of various bodies that encourage institutional investors to act as good stewards of their members' capital through the integration of ESG factors and active ownership (monitoring, engagement, and voting) practices. The national investment bodies support that:

- responsible investing is a positive force influencing corporate behavior through encouraging responsible actions;
- responsible investment is more than negative screening;
- engagement can be a powerful tool to change corporate behavior;
- promoting ESG issues in the companies in which we invest serves both parts of our mandate: to generate good financial returns while honouring the values of our organizations and the denomination.

United Church of Christ (UCC)
United Church Funds
www.ucfunds.org

Established in 1909, United Church Funds (UCF) offers a family of thirteen professionally managed, well-diversified, and socially responsible investment funds to over 1,000 churches, conferences, associations, and other ministries of the United Church of Christ. At present, UCF manages over $800 million in assets—from small church reserve accounts to some of the denomination's historic endowments.

Investors in UCF's funds benefit from a range of advantages, including

- faith-based investing and endowment solutions
- diversified funds that span the spectrum of risk and return
- competitive performance and attractive fee structures
- more than 100 years of supporting the mission of our clients
- nonprofit, values-aligned, and committed to improving the world

Investing with United Church Funds, churches and other UCC ministries enjoy the best practices of modern portfolio management while remaining faithful to the values of the United Church of Christ. We seek solid investment performance with a purpose: to make more money available for your ministry.

United Methodist

For a United Methodist foundation that serves your local regional conference, please check with your local regional leadership.

UMC Foundation Investment Management
www.investumc.org

UMC Foundation Investment Management is built on a solid foundation of stewardship and generosity—reflected in our mission. Started in 2000 as the United Methodist Church Foundation, we collaborated with agencies, foundations, and institutions of the United Methodist Church, with a faithful calling and commitment to creating a better world. At the time, the United Methodist Church Foundation had two main functions: to work with partners to create lasting financial legacies through gifts and endowments, and to invest and manage those funds. In 2014, the fundraising and gift development component of the Foundation separated from the investment management division. With investment management becoming our primary focus, our team now concentrates on offering expert institutional investment management with innovative, personalized service.

Organizations That Can Help You Get Involved in Socially Responsible Investing and Encourage Giving

Interfaith Center on Corporate Responsibility (ICCR)
www.iccr.org

Mission: Shareholders calling the world's most powerful companies to address their impact on the world's most vulnerable communities. (See ICCR's history on this book's website: *www.churchpublishing.org/faithfulinvesting*)

Ceres
www.ceres.org

Ceres is a sustainability nonprofit organization working with the most influential investors and companies to build leadership and drive solutions throughout the economy. Through powerful networks and advocacy, Ceres tackles the world's biggest sustainability challenges, including climate change, water scarcity and pollution, and inequitable workplaces.

For personal SRI considerations, see chapter 11.
For Impact or Community Investment resources, see chapter 8.

Organizations That Can Help You Raise Funds

Check with your own denomination or denominational foundation for additional resources for raising financial resources.

Ecumenical Stewardship Center (ESC)
www.stewardshipresources.org

As *a Network for Growing Stewards*, the Ecumenical Stewardship Center helps the church thrive as it learns to live generously. The Ecumenical Stewardship provides resources for a year-round emphasis on stewardship and generosity, materials for annual stewardship campaigns, events to build a stewardship and generosity toolbox, capital and major gift campaign consulting, and professional networking opportunities. The *Giving: Growing Joyful Stewards in Your Congregation* magazine contains thoughtful, practical, and inspirational content for your church leadership, written by thought leaders and practitioners from throughout the church. Access dozens of resources with a generosity365 subscription. Learn more at *https://stewardshipresources. org/subscribe/generosity365-subscription-for-congregations/*.

For Episcopal Churches
The Episcopal Network for Stewardship (TENS)
www.tens.org

TENS' vision is to provide training and resources for stewardship leaders across the Episcopal Church and beyond around the following core competencies: training clergy and lay leaders in the spirituality of money, and the skills required to address questions of money in the congregation; providing targeted stewardship leadership training for clergy and seminarians, at seminaries and at the diocesan level, including both the theology and the practice of stewardship; mentoring a new generation of stewardship leaders, with special attention to young adults, generation Xers, and newly ordained clergy; developing and utilizing methods of providing resources and using web-based and other electronic techniques. TENS offers training days, workshops, and consulting in addition to online stewardship resources.

Project Resource
www.project-resource.org

Project Resource is an initiative adapted to enable an entirely new culture in all aspects of financial development: spiritual, organizational, and managerial. It is designed to train leaders how to return to their diocese to lead others within the diocese's culture, geography, and cultural realities as they develop leaders and raise money. It is also configured to teach effective use of model documents archived online for easy teaching access.

Contributors

James W. Murphy, CFRE, Managing Editor/Contributing Author

Jim Murphy is managing program director at the Episcopal Church Foundation. He oversees ECF's financial resources programs: endowment management, planned giving, and donor solutions, including ECF's donor-advised fund program. During his tenure he has overseen the endowment program's growth from $80 million to nearly $400 million in assets under management. He works with congregations, dioceses, and other Episcopal organizations to grow their endowments and enhance and develop their planned giving programs and various philanthropic efforts and resources. Jim holds a certificate in fundraising from New York University's School of Continuing and Professional Studies, an MA in Christian spirituality from the General Theological Seminary, and a BS from NYU's Stern School of Business. Jim is a member of the Association of Fundraising Professionals and is a Certified Fund Raising Executive.

Byrd Bonner, Esq.

Byrd Bonner is former president of the UMC Foundation and a licensed Texas attorney in private practice in family law and child protection. He served as the president/CEO of the United Methodist Church Foundation from 2000 to 2017. Byrd served the Interfaith Center on Corporate Responsibility as vice chair of the board of directors, and as chair of its investment committee and development committee. At the ICCR table, Byrd worked on forums relating to climate change, corporate governance, and human trafficking, and negotiated significant governance charter changes in board diversity. His primary focus for the Foundation was to encourage the inclusion of women and persons of color on corporate boards. Other priority issues were the fight against human trafficking, greenhouse gas emission reduction, EEO reporting, and reduction of access to violent video gaming by youth and children. Building on ICCR's legacy, Byrd's passion was promoting ESG principles in fiduciary practices on both sides of the table. Byrd remains an individual member of the Socially Responsible Investment Coalition, and chairs the board of his local United Methodist congregation's foundation in San Antonio, Texas.

Tim Brennan

Tim Brennan is treasurer and chief financial officer of the Unitarian Universalist Association and has served in that role since June 2006. In addition to overseeing the department of finance, he oversees the Association's assets, including the UU Common Endowment Fund, the UU Organizations Retirement Fund, the charitable gift funds, and outside trusts with combined assets of approximately $600 million. He is a member of the UUA's investment committee, socially responsible investing committee, retirement plan committee, and the UUA Health Plan Board of Trustees. Tim came to the UUA after seven years with Ceres, the national network of institutional investors working to advance corporate responsibility for the environment. As senior director, development and communications, he worked with major environmental organizations, religious investors, the SRI community, and major pension funds on issues such as climate change and corporate sustainability disclosure. In addition, Tim spent seven years working for a New York investment company and has many years of experience in nonprofit financial management. He currently serves on the board of the Interfaith Center for Corporate Responsibility. Tim holds an MBA from the Wharton School of the University of Pennsylvania in finance and accounting.

Sister Patricia Daly, OP

Sister Patricia Daly, OP, is a Dominican Sister of Caldwell, New Jersey, and has worked in corporate responsibility and socially responsible investing for over forty years. After almost twenty-four years, Pat recently concluded her tenure as executive director of the Tri-State Coalition for Responsible Investment, an organization of forty Roman Catholic Dioceses and Congregations of Women and Men primarily in the New York metropolitan area. Pat has invited companies to address issues of human rights, labor, ecological concerns, equality, and international debt and capital flows, and played a role in positioning the agenda of global warming into the priorities of corporate America. In addition to representing her congregation before corporations, Pat serves on the advisory boards of Lamont-Doherty Earth Observatory, the climate science arm of Columbia University's Earth Institute, and JANA Partners, the first hedge fund to implement corporate engagement and socially responsible principles. Pat initiated the recent launch of Climate Finance investment fund that works to implement the UN Sustainable Development Goals. She is the proud recipient of the 2014 Joan Bavaria Award presented by Ceres and Trillium Asset Management and the 2017 Legacy Award presented by ICCR, and holds honorary doctorates from William Paterson University and Duquesne University.

The Rev. Séamus P. Finn, OMI

The Rev. Séamus P. Finn, OMI, is responsible for the Faith Consistent Investing program for the Oblate Investment Pastoral Trust (www.oiptrust.org). He represents the Missionary Oblates (OMI) at the Interfaith Center on Corporate Responsibility, where he serves as the board chair. His responsibilities include directing the implementation of the responsible investment policies of the OIP, including the active engagement as shareholders with individual corporations that are in the portfolio.

He participates in various roundtable multistakeholder discussions across different industry sectors, as well as in conferences and symposia that are convened at the Vatican and by other international faith forums on the Sustainable Development Goals, impact investing, and the promotion of responsible mining for the common good. He has also been a member of the Justice/Peace and Integrity of Creation (JPIC) ministry team of the Missionary Oblates of Mary Immaculate since 1986 and is currently director of the USP OMI JPIC office (www.omiusajpic.org). The JPIC team is also responsible for the multistakeholder advocacy public policy program of the Missionary Oblates with US and global public institutions.

Bobbi Hannigan

Bobbi Hannigan served as the treasury manager at Catholic Extension, overseeing portfolios in excess of $250 million. She has been at the forefront of monitoring investment managers' compliance to the Roman Catholic Church's socially responsible investing guidelines. Her responsibilities entailed implementing investment strategies that seek to avoid participation in harmful activities and identify those promoting the common good while also meeting fiduciary obligations to over fifty-five bishops. She was a key contributor to the 2017 MSCI ESG thought leader research paper "Trends in Catholic Investment Strategies." She holds an Investment Foundations Certificate from CFA and is an active participant in SRI/ESG and faith-based investment forums as well as the Chicago-based Women Investment Professionals. Bobbi recently left Catholic Extension to join the Cristo Rey Network, headquartered in Chicago, Illinois.

Lisa Hinds

Lisa Hinds is a senior vice president and nonprofit practice leader for a global alternative asset manager. She brings over twenty-five years of experience in client portfolio management, institutional securities trading, and investment banking. She currently serves as vice chair of the board and chair of the investment committee of United Church Funds, the institutional investment ministry of the United Church of Christ. She is a former deacon, trustee, and chair of the finance committee of The Riverside Church in the City of New York. Ms. Hinds holds an MBA from the Fuqua School of Business at Duke University, a master of arts in law and diplomacy from the Fletcher School at Tufts University, and a bachelor of science from Northeastern University.

Joseph M. Kinard

Joseph M. Kinard is chair of the Presbyterian Church (USA) Committee on Mission Responsibility Through Investment (MRTI), which was created in 1971 to advance the church's mission through the financial resources (approximately $10 billion dollars) entrusted to it. MRTI implements the PCUSA policies on socially responsible investing (also called faith-based investing) by engaging corporations in which the church owns stock. Priorities for MRTI include: pursuit of peace; racial, social, and economic justice; environmental responsibility; and securing women's rights.

During his tenure as board member of the Presbyterian Church (USA) Board of Pensions, Mr. Kinard served on the CEO Search; Investment; Board Development and Governance; Social Responsibility; and Church Relations Committees. In addition, Mr. Kinard served as a reviewer of the Presbyterian Church (USA) Foundation investment strategy. He is an acknowledged thought leader in Corporate Socially Responsible/Impact Investing (CSR II), having spoken at Institutional Investor Summits sponsored by the New York Stock Exchange, NASDAQ, Thomson Reuters, Institutional Real Estate Investors, and High Water Women's Investing for Impact Symposium. He was also guest lecturer at the University of the South Babson Center for Global Commerce and Yale University School of Management Impact Investing Conference.

Mr. Kinard, through his company The Kinard Group, LLC, has helped companies in obtaining venture capital, angel, and mezzanine financing representing both capital funds and their portfolio companies. In 2018, Mr. Kinard was inducted into the National Association of Securities Professionals (NASP) Wall Street Hall of Fame. NASP is the oldest organization in America supporting women and minorities in the financial services industry.

Kathryn McCloskey

Katie McCloskey is the director of social responsibility for United Church Funds, which invests on behalf of United Church of Christ churches and institutions. With extensive experience in the not-for-profit and humanitarian fields, she holds a BA in women's studies and literature from the University of Virginia. Katie has previously worked for the Institute for Women's Policy Research and the Corporate Executive Board. Katie currently serves as vice chair of the board of the Interfaith Center on Corporate Responsibility (ICCR) and as a convener of the Climate Solutions Impact Investing group. She has convened the Jubilee Assembly, an interfaith group of investors searching for impact investing opportunities.

The Rev. Aimee Moiso

Aimee Moiso is a minister in the Presbyterian Church (USA) and a PhD candidate at Vanderbilt University in Nashville, Tennessee. Her dissertation focuses on the challenges and possibilities of preaching in times of polarization and division. During the final year of her studies, she is serving as a practical theologian in residence for the Presbyterian Foundation. Before beginning her doctoral program, Aimee was director of ecumenical and interfaith ministries at Santa Clara University in California. She also has degrees from San Francisco Theological Seminary and the Bossey Ecumenical Institute in Geneva, Switzerland. When she has time, Aimee loves to be in the garden helping to coax life out of the dirt, or in the kitchen pulling baked goods out of the oven. She lives in Nashville with her husband, Rev. Nolan Huizenga, also a Presbyterian minister.

Mark A. Regier

Mark A. Regier is vice president of Stewardship Investing, Mennonite Foundation, and Everence Financial and has been involved in the field of ethical and socially responsible investing at Everence for more than twenty years. He oversees the company's work in socially responsible investing (including investment screening, ESG integration, proxy voting, corporate engagement, and community investing). In addition, Mark works with products and programs throughout Everence to strengthen their creative integration of faith and finances. In 2015, Mark assumed leadership of the sales and marketing efforts for Praxis Mutual Funds.

Mark has served as a member of the board of directors for the US Social Investment Forum, the Interfaith Center on Corporate Responsibility, Partners for the Common Good, the International Working Group, the Isaiah Fund for Disaster Recovery Investing, and the Highland Good Steward SRI hedge fund. In 2006, Mark received the SRI Service Award, the US social investment industry's highest honor.

With over twenty-five years of service to the church and a background in ethics and theological studies, Mark is often a resource to national and international media and organizations on faith-based and community investing issues.

Greg Rousos

Greg Rousos is president of New Covenant Trust Company and executive vice president and chief operating officer of the Presbyterian Foundation. New Covenant Trust Company manages over $1.7 billion in assets on behalf of Presbyterian parishes and institutions, as well as over $20 million in donor-advised fund assets and $50 million in life income gifts. Greg is a certified public accountant and a Certified Financial Planner professional, as well as a graduate of Ohio State University. Greg has been happily married to his wife, Jenny, for over thirty years. They are blessed with two wonderful daughters and their husbands. In their spare time, Greg and Jenny enjoy traveling and their two dogs, Preston and Bailey.

Carsten W. Sierck, JD

Carsten W. Sierck, JD, is program director for endowment management, planned giving, and donor solutions at Episcopal Church Foundation. She advises churches, dioceses, schools, and church-related organizations on how to structure, manage, use, and grow their endowments. She also consults with lay and clergy leaders considering socially responsible investing at their churches. Previously, Carsten held positions at financial planning and wealth management firms in Cleveland, Ohio. She also founded her own firm, where she worked to improve the financial lives of families in transition. Earlier in her career, she practiced law in New York City and Washington, DC. Carsten is a graduate of Columbia University and the University of Virginia Law School. A lifelong Episcopalian, she attended the National Cathedral School in Washington, DC, for fourteen years.

The Rev. William Somplatsky-Jarman

The Rev. William Somplatsky-Jarman served as the primary staff of the Presbyterian Church (USA) faith-based investment committee for thirty-two years. During that time, he coordinated hundreds of corporate dialogues, addressed numerous stockholder meetings, and authored articles on a wide variety of socially responsible investment issues. During his career, he served on the board of the Interfaith Center on Corporate Responsibility (ICCR), which gave him a Lifetime Achievement Award in 2016. Other board and leadership service included Ceres, Interfaith Worker Justice, the Eco-Justice Working Group of the National Council of Churches, World Council of Churches Working Group on Climate Change, Commission on Religion in Appalachia, and Coalition for Justice in the Maquiladoras. Rev. Somplatsky-Jarman has led experiential study trips to Appalachia, US/Mexico border, and the Brazilian Amazon. He graduated cum laude from Bethany College in West Virginia and Yale Divinity School, where he was awarded the Mersick Prize for effective public address, especially in preaching. He now resides in Utah, where he and his spouse, Carol, enjoy exploring the red rock canyon country.